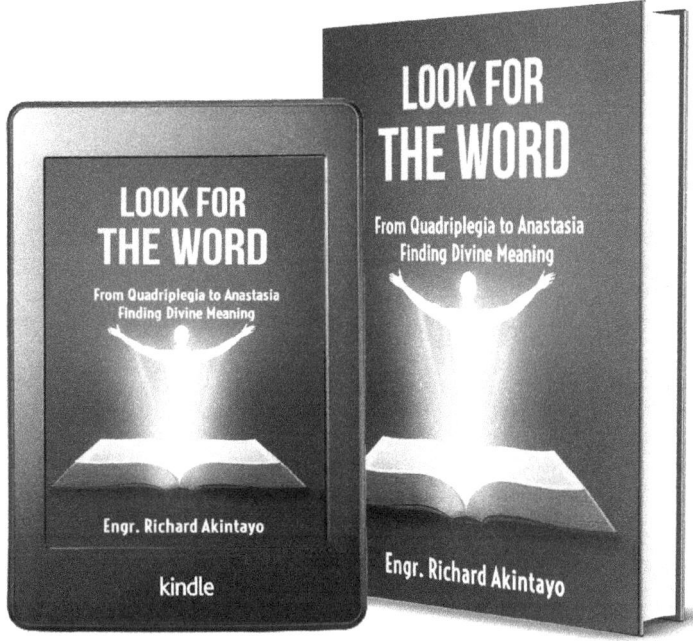

From the Author

Thank you so much for purchasing this book! If you have found it helpful, we would greatly appreciate it if you could take a moment to leave an honest review on Amazon. Your feedback will assist others in discovering this book and, hopefully, reaping its benefits as well.

ENGR. RICHARD AKINTAYO

LOOK FOR THE WORD

Copyright © 2025 Engr. Richard Akintayo

ISBN: 978-1-64301-071-7

Library of Congress Control Number: 2025928059

NOTICE OF RIGHTS
All Rights Reserved. Reproduction of this material, in whole or part, by whatever means, without the express written consent by the author is not permitted, and is unlawful according to current copyright laws of the United States of America to do so.

BIBLE REFERENCE
Scriptures are taken from various translations of the Bible as indicated, except otherwise.

AUTHOR'S CONTACT:
rakintayo54@gmail.com

INTERIOR DESIGNED AND FORMATTED BY REHOBOTH HOUSE
COVER DESIGNED BY Engr. Richard Akintayo

PUBLISHED IN THE UNITED STATES OF AMERICA
By Rehoboth House, Chicago
rehobothhouseonline.com
info@rehobothhouseonline.com
rehobothpublishing@gmail.com

PRINTED IN THE UNITED STATES OF AMERICA

TABLE OF CONTENTS

Dedication..*v*
Acknowledgment..*vii*
Preface..*xi*
Introduction..*xiii*

SECTION 1: WORD AND SPIRIT

CHAPTER 1: *The Word Before Words*..1

CHAPTER 2: *The Word That Speaks Creation*.....................................5

CHAPTER 3: *The Word Made Flesh*..9

CHAPTER 4: *The Word in the Wilderness*...13

CHAPTER 5: *The Word That Heals*...17

CHAPTER 6: *The Word in Us*...21

CHAPTER 7: *The Word That Waits*..27

CHAPTER 8: *The Word That Sends*..33

CHAPTER 9: *The Word and the Spirit — Divine Partnership*............39

SECTION 2: FROM QUADRIPLEGIA TO ANASTASIA

CHAPTER 10: *Quadriplegia, The Stillness Where the Word Whispers*............53

CHAPTER 11: *Transformation, The Word as Healing and Identity*................61

CHAPTER 12: *Anastasia, The Word That Raises*...71

CHAPTER 13: *Individual Experience, When the Word Speaks Your Name*....77

CHAPTER 14: *Conclusion, Look for the Word, Live the Word*.......................99

EPILOGUE: *Poetry of the Paralyzed*...105

NOTES AND REFERENCE INDEX..113

Dedication

I dedicate this book first to the One who heals, restores, and calls us by name, to the Lord God Almighty, whose mercy endures forever; to Jesus Christ, the Living Word, who sent His healing and bore my infirmities; and to the Holy Spirit, my Comforter and Counselor, whose constant presence and divine power are the divine inspiration behind these pages. Let this inspire hope that God's healing is always available to those who seek it, and let it fill you with confidence in His divine guidance.

To my beloved wife, Maureen Olayinka Akintayo: your steadfast love, intercession, and unshakable faith carried me through the valley. This book is your testimony as much as it is mine. Your courage shapes every chapter, and may generations rise to call you blessed.

This work is also dedicated to the listener in stillness, the one who has wondered whether the body is a mistake. The body is not an error; it is the Creator's first message, formed from dust, given life, and revealing God's intention. Yet when the body fails, we can feel alone or forsaken. Scripture shows us, however, that weakness can be a calling rather than a punishment. In the paralyzed limbs of the man lowered through the roof, Jesus saw faith. Even broken bodies, like Christ's after the resurrection, can inspire belief and carry glory. Be encouraged to listen for God's voice in your own moments of silence and weakness.

So, I dedicate this book to every soul who has felt immobilized, physically, emotionally, or spiritually, and yet has dared to listen for the whisper of God. To those searching for meaning in suffering and finding the Word speaking life to them. May you discover your divine identity and walk boldly in His resurrection light, renewed and strengthened.

Richard Akintayo.

Acknowledgments

I begin by giving thanks to God Almighty for His grace, mercy, and abundant blessings upon my life. I honor the Lord Jesus Christ, whose Word healed me, and I thank the Holy Spirit for enforcing that healing and inspiring this book from its very beginning to its completion. May this acknowledgment remind you of God's unwavering support and inspire trust in His divine care, reassuring you that He continues to speak and guide you.

To my beloved wife of over forty years, Maureen Olayinka, my heart overflows with gratitude. Your unwavering support, full-time care, and prayerful presence by my hospital bedside for sixty-six days and beyond were a living testimony of your love for me and your faith in God. May you continually reap the rewards of your labor of love.

To my children—Olawale, Olamide, Oladapo, and Olufolakemi—thank you for your care, support, and strength during that difficult season. May the Lord bless you richly, supply all your needs, and grant you long life in good health. To my daughters—Lavender, Mathilda, and Eniola—you are truly blessed and highly favored of the Lord, and I remain grateful for the joy you bring into our lives.

I am deeply grateful to my pastors—Rev. Chris Okotie, and Pastor Tunde & Pastor (Mrs.) Layide Bakare—for their spiritual covering, prayers, and love. Your faithfulness inspires confidence and reassurance, and I thank you for standing with me in faith.

To my in-laws—Tom & Irene Wachira, Tayo and Tutu Ayeni, Mrs. Ireti Abimbola, Mr. Femi Akinbola, Mrs. Titi Lawani, Mrs. Toyin Akinbola, Mrs. Ajinomo, and Grandmas Ayeni and Sanusi—thank you for your prayers, hospitality, and kindness. Your support of my family and me during this period was invaluable, making you feel like a vital part of our journey and strengthening your sense of belonging in God's family.

I also acknowledge, with deep appreciation, friends whose loyalty, presence, and prayers sustained us. Dr. Fred and Mrs. Tutu Tega, your steadfast support before and throughout my hospitalization and recovery meant the world to us. Dr. Gboyega Oke, thank you for journeying with us to Atlanta and standing by us with strength and compassion. Mr. Lekan and Mrs. Lara Adebiyi, your visits, prayers, and love were unrelenting. Engr. Bayo & Mrs. Toks Adebowale, and Engr. Ayo & Mrs. Bunmi Lawson, your friendship and kindness have been a continuous blessing.

My special thanks go to Mr. Fisayo and Mrs. Shola Omojokun for faithfully visiting with the children and taking us to Victory Church Norcross every Sunday—may the Lord reward your labor of love. I am grateful to Dr. Biodun Kuku and his daughter Tobi for their prayers and visits; to Mrs. Maryam Uwais, whose visits from Nigeria, along with Abdallah's kindness, touched us deeply; and to Mr. Mike Igbokwe, SAN, whose sharing of scriptural references strengthened my faith and healing. I also appreciate Mrs. Bola Odusi and Mrs. Ikepo Osawaye for their relentless hope, visits, and robust prayer chain; Mr. Dotun

Adeseye for traveling from Houston to see us; Anne Coker Bremmer and Peju Coker, whose phone calls and prayers were soothing; Captain Tunji Shelle, for his timely prayers and scriptural messages; and Engr. Tunde Shitta Bey, for his message of hope and encouragement.

I also acknowledge my beloved Household of GOD brethren, Gbenga & Ronke, Jerry, Arthur, Omosede Osidele, Emeka, Debbie, Seyi, Joe, Henry, Tetteh, and many others, thank you for your love, prayers, and encouragement.

Finally, I extend my heartfelt gratitude to Biola Balogun, my sisters, every member of my extended family, and friends and well-wishers whose encouragement and prayers helped me overcome the challenges along the way. Your kindness, in ways both seen and unseen, will never be forgotten. May the Lord, who sees in secret, openly reward you all.

Look For The Word

Personal Notes ———————————————

Preface

Wherever silence exists, a Word is waiting to be found-whether through Scripture, prayer, divine impressions, or inner conviction. Learning to discern God's voice from other influences and trusting in His guidance encourages obedience and deepens our relationship with Him, guiding us toward our purpose.

We examine, scrutinize, and study to find the Word. The Word may be written or spoken, and often comes through prayer, meditation, or promptings of the Holy Spirit. In many traditions, the spoken Word carries power; it becomes a vessel of destiny and prophecy. To seek the Word is to find the utterance that unlocks understanding. The right Word can shift paradigms, reframe a challenge, ignite a movement, or define a brand. It may be hidden in data, buried in emotion, or waiting in quiet reflection—but once found, it guides us like a compass pointing to true north.

We look for the Word in poems, proverbs, and policies; in dreams, documents, visions, and revelations. We search for the Word that speaks truth, carries legacy, and dares to imagine a better world. It is a call to look for the Word—not just any word, but the one that unlocks purpose, bridges generations, and carries the weight of legacy. To seek the Word is to pursue wisdom, honor heritage, and shape the future through faithful speech. Words guide us. They become the compass that points toward transformation. A mentor does not merely advise; she speaks life into dormant dreams. To build legacy, the Word becomes a signature—the story etched into policy. It is about veracity, not just visibility.

The Word is the act of choosing clarity over clutter and depth over decoration. In the age of AI, where algorithms echo but do not empathize, the human Word remains sacred. It is our ethical anchor and our cultural code. Yet the Word is elusive. It hides in the folds of memory, in the rhythm of tradition, and in the pulse of innovation. It demands patience, humility, and courage. Sometimes it arrives as thunder; other times, as dew. But when it comes, it clarifies everything.

So look for the Word not only in books and speeches, but also in proverbs, in people, and within yourself, where it may already be waiting.

This book is a Christian exploration of divine meaning, sharing my encounter with the life-giving WORD.

God's spoken Word sustained me through a catastrophic health crisis—from quadriplegia to "Anastasia."

That journey is chronicled in Section Two, Chapters 10–13. It is more than a personal story; it is a clear summons to engage. It is a call to listen with the ear of the spirit, to discern God's voice amid the noise of the world, and to respond not merely with understanding, but with obedience. Take note f the following:

- *The Word convicts*
- *The Word comforts*
- *The Word heals*
- *The Word calls*

Introduction

There are three kinds of words to watch out for: human words, the devil's words, and GOD's Words. Words are powerful—they penetrate the heart. There is power in their words, power in our words to ourselves, and power in our words to others. Death and life are in the power of the tongue, and those who love it will eat of its fruit.

GOD is a speaking God. He has given us the ability to use words, freedom of speech. But we must not use the devil's words. Replace faulty words with GOD's Words.

GOD's Word refers to the written or spoken message of GOD, as well as the message of GOD revealed in the person of JESUS CHRIST, called the Word.

Written Message of GOD

GOD did not leave His people to guess His will; He chose to have His commands, promises, and covenants written down for all generations. Through written revelation, His Word can be read, studied, and preserved, whether in stone, scrolls, or Scripture. These writings become a stable reference point for faith, obedience, and spiritual growth.

The Ten Commandments

Exodus 31:18 — When the Lord finished speaking to Moses on Mount Sinai, He gave him two tablets of the covenant law, the tablets of stone inscribed by the finger of GOD.

Prophetic writings — Books like Isaiah, Jeremiah, and Ezekiel contain messages GOD instructed prophets to write down for His people.

The Bible as a whole — A written message from GOD through human authors guided by the Holy Spirit *(2 Timothy 3:16).*

Spoken Message of GOD

Long before printing presses and digital Bibles, God's Word was proclaimed aloud—preached in synagogues, declared by prophets, and spoken by Jesus Himself. Spoken messages carry urgency and immediacy, often confronting people in real time with God's truth. These declarations, later recorded in Scripture, still speak with the same authority and power today.

Examples of God Speaking Through Scripture:

- Jesus declares He is the fulfillment of Isaiah's prophecy *(Luke 4:16 -21)*
- Paul quotes Hosea to show prophecy fulfillment *(Romans 9:25–26)*
- Peter's Pentecost sermon *(Acts 2:14-36)*
- King Josiah repents *(2 Kings 22:8–20)*
- God instructs the Israelites through the Law *(Amos 5)*
- Jeremiah reminds Israel of God's Law *(Jeremiah 6:16)*

Introduction

God Speaking in Dreams

Dreams are one of the quiet ways God speaks when our bodies are at rest, but our spirits remain reachable. In dreams, He may reveal warnings, future events, or confirmations that we could easily miss while distracted in daily life. These nighttime encounters often carry symbols and scenes that invite prayerful interpretation.

> *Job 33:14–16 NKJV "For God may speak in one way, or in another, yet man does not perceive it. In a dream, in a vision of the night, when deep sleep falls upon men, while slumbering on their beds, then He opens the ears of men, and seals their instruction."*

Dreams occur while sleeping.

- Joseph's dreams (Genesis 37)
- Jacob's dream (Genesis 28:10–22)
- Pharaoh's dream (Genesis 41)
- God's Word to Abimelech (Genesis 20:1–7)
- Pharaoh's servant and the baker (Genesis 40)
- Nebuchadnezzar's (Daniel 2)
- The Wise Men are warned (Matthew 1:1–12)
- Joseph's escape to Egypt with baby Jesus (Matthew 2:13–18)
- Daniel interprets a dream (Daniel 4)

God Speaking in Visions

Visions come while a person is awake, yet taken into a spiritual encounter where God reveals what natural eyes cannot see. In visions, He may reveal His glory, unfold history, or assign specific tasks to individuals and nations. These experiences often mark turning points in a person's life or in God's story.

Visions can occur while awake

- Ezekiel's vision of the glory of the Lord (Ezekiel 1)
- The Lord's covenant with Abraham (Genesis 15)
- Isaiah's commission (Isaiah 6)
- Ananias' vision to visit Paul (Acts 9:10–16)
- Cornelius' vision of an angel (Acts 10:1–7)

God Speaking Directly to People

At key moments in history, God has spoken directly to men and women in words they could clearly hear and understand. These encounters often come with holy fear, deep assurance, or explicit instruction that cannot be ignored. When God speaks directly, He leaves no doubt that He knows our name, our situation, and our destiny.

- Moses and the burning bush (Exodus 3)
- God speaks to Samuel (1 Samuel 3)
- Saul's conversion (Acts 9:1–19)
- God defends Moses (Numbers 12:1–9)
- Joshua is called to lead (Joshua 1:1–19)
- David dialogues with God (2 Samuel 2:1)
- Jesus is baptized (Matthew 3:16–17)
- The Transfiguration (Luke 9:28–36)
- Moses parts the Red Sea (Exodus 14)
- God speaks to Job (Job 38)

God Speaking Through the Holy Spirit

In the New Testament era, the Holy Spirit is God's living presence within believers, guiding, correcting, and comforting from the inside out. He speaks through inner promptings, spiritual impressions, and a quiet witness that aligns with Scripture. When we learn to recognize His voice, our steps, timing, and decisions become more closely aligned with God's will.

- Paul and the man from Macedonia (Acts 16:6–10)
- Philip and the Ethiopian official (Acts 8:29)
- Barnabas and Saul are called (Acts 13:1–3)
- Paul is warned of hardship (Acts 20:22–24)
- Bezalel, the artisan (Exodus 31:1–11)
- The three men and Peter (Acts 10:19–20)
- Nehemiah senses a stirring (Nehemiah 2)

God Speaking Through Angelic Messengers

Angels are God's messengers, sent at crucial times to deliver His Word, bring reassurance, or give direction. Their appearances in Scripture often come at turning points—before battles, births, or major assignments. Through angels, God reminds His people that heaven is actively involved in earthly affairs.

- An angel strengthens Gideon (Judges 6:11–24)
- An angel comes to Mary (Luke 1:26–38)
- Hagar meets an angel (Genesis 16:7–12)
- An angel stops Abraham (Genesis 22)
- Jesus' birth is announced to the shepherds (Luke 2:8–14)

God Speaking Through Prophets, Words of Knowledge, and Wise Counsel

God uses people filled with His Spirit to speak timely words into our lives, communities, and nations. Prophets, spiritual gifts, and wise counselors help us hear what God is saying when we might otherwise miss it. Their words must align with Scripture, but when they do, they can confirm direction, expose sin, or release hope.

- Nathan speaks to David (2 Samuel 12:1–14)
- Samuel speaks God's judgment to Saul (1 Samuel 15)
- Elijah announces a drought (1 Kings 17:1)
- Elisha reveals enemy plans (2 Kings 6:12)
- John the Baptist declares Jesus as the Messiah (John 1:29–31)

God Speaking Through Nature, Signs, Wonders, and the Supernatural

Creation itself is a canvas where God's voice can be seen in color, pattern, and power. At times, He uses unusual signs, wonders, and supernatural events to get our attention and underscore His covenant and glory. These moments remind us that the God who made the world still rules it and can interrupt the natural order to speak.

- A cloud and fire guide the Israelites (Exodus 13:21–22)
- Balaam's donkey speaks (Numbers 22:21–41)
- Gideon's fleece (Judges 6:36–40)
- Thunder, lightning, and trumpet blast (Exodus 19:16–25)
- The rainbow covenant (Genesis 9:1–17)
- The earth shakes after Jesus' crucifixion (Matthew 27:51)

Each chapter invites you to seek the Word of God in unexpected places—in stillness, in brokenness, and in the quiet unfolding of your spiritual identity. Along the way, you will encounter Scripture, reflection, and Holy Spirit–breathed insights, all designed to guide you gently yet powerfully into deeper communion with God.

This introduction, and every chapter that follows, concludes with a prayer—a sacred pause to respond, receive, and rest in the presence of the Word. These moments of prayer are invitations to move from mere reading into encounter, from information into transformation.

Prayer: Listening for the Word

Pray this aloud as you prepare to listen for God's Word and respond to what He speaks to your heart.

Lord God,
You are the speaking God,
From burning bush to whisper,
From thunder on Sinai to the still, small voice within.

You have given us the gift of words,
To bless, to build, to believe,
To comfort, to correct, to create.
But beyond speech,
You offer revelation.
You invite me to listen,
Not just with my ears, but with my spirit.

In a world of noise and distraction,
Teach me to hear Your Word.
Not the words of fear, or pride, or confusion,
But the Word that brings life,
The Word that heals,
The Word that calls me by name.

Let me discern Your voice among many.
Let me replace the enemy's lies with Your truth.
Let my mouth agree with heaven.
Let me speak what You speak:
Words that carry grace, wisdom, and legacy.

Holy Spirit, guide me into all truth.
Illuminate the Word.
Interpret the silence.
Reveal the things to come.
Let me not just read Scripture,
But encounter the Living Word.
Let me not just memorize verses,
But be transformed by them.

Jesus, Word made flesh,
Speak again into my heart.
Shape my thoughts, my speech, my story.
Let my life echo Your voice,
So that others hear You through me.
Amen.

Personal Notes

SECTION ONE

Word And Spirit

CHAPTER 1

The Word Before Words

John 1:1 KJV — "In the beginning was the Word, and the Word was with God, and the Word was God."

Before time ticked its first moment and before light pierced the void, there was the Word, eternal, living, divine. From this foundation, we trace the source of all creation. The Word is not a mere sound but a Person; not just language, but Logos, the logic, meaning, and heartbeat of all that would ever exist. Scripture reveals the eternal nature of Christ not only as a messenger, but as the very message; not merely present at creation, but preexistent, divine, and active. Before beginnings began, the Word was not formed, not created, but Eternal. The Word was with God, and the Word was God.

This is Jesus:
- The voice behind "Let there be light."
- The breath that stirred dust into life.
- The presence that hovered over the deep.
- He is not just the speaker—He is the speech.
- Not just the messenger—He is the message.

> *Genesis 1:2 KJV — "And the earth was without form, and void; and darkness was upon the face of the deep. And the Spirit of God moved upon the face of the waters."*

This verse sets the stage for divine creation, not with order but with chaos, preparing us for the moment when the Word intervenes. It is the moment before the Word speaks, when the Spirit hovers, waiting to activate the voice of God. It is a scene rich with mystery and power. Before form, there was formlessness; before beauty, there was a void; before light, there was darkness. Yet the Spirit of God was already there—hovering, moving, preparing. It is the sacred pause before creation, the breath before the Word, the moment when chaos is pregnant with possibility.

> *Hebrews 1:3 KJV — "Who being the brightness of his glory, and the express image of his person, and upholding all things by the word of his power, when he had by himself purged our sins, sat down on the right hand of the Majesty on high."*

Here we see Christ not only as the agent of creation but also as the sustainer, redeemer, and the exact revelation of God's glory. Jesus is the brightness of God's glory—He does not merely reflect it; He radiates it. He is the express image of God's nature, not a shadow or suggestion, but the exact imprint of His being. He upholds all things not by strain or struggle, but by the word of His power. This Word does not simply create; it sustains. It not only speaks beginnings; it carries them to completion. And it does not merely shape the cosmos; it purges sin and then sits enthroned at the right hand of the Majesty on high.

> *Psalm 33:6 KJV — "By the word of the Lord were the heavens made; and all the host of them by the breath of his mouth."*

This verse is a majestic declaration of divine creativity, linking God's act of speaking to the very existence of the cosmos. The heavens were not constructed by human effort; the Word of the Lord called them forth. The stars did not ignite by accident; they were breathed into brilliance by His mouth. The Word of the Lord is not passive—it is powerful. It does not merely describe reality; it defines it. The breath of His mouth does more than stir the wind; it animates galaxies. And this same Word and Breath formed you. You are not an accident; you are the result of divine utterance.

> *Revelation 19:13 KJV — "And he was clothed with a vesture dipped in blood: and his name is called The Word of God."*

In this climactic revelation, Christ is unveiled as The Word of God—not only as Creator, but as Warrior, Judge, and King, bringing the story full circle. The Word that once spoke light into darkness now rides in glory, clothed in sacrifice. His robe bears the mark of redemption—bloodshed, victory won. He is not only the Word of creation; He is the Word of consummation. He is not just the beginning; He is the end. His name is not a metaphor; it is His identity: The Word of God. The same Word that formed the world now brings justice, redemption, and final victory.

— *Reflection Point* —

Before creation, before language, before breath, there was the Word. And the Spirit hovered, ready to activate what the Word would say. The Word and the Spirit move together in perfect unity. This book is a journey to rediscover that Word, not only in Scripture, but in silence, in suffering, in service, and in the hidden corners of our stories. The divine narrative did not end in Genesis; it continues in our own experiences as we learn to recognize the Word at work in and through us.

Prayer of Awe: The Word Before Words

Eternal Word,
Before syllables were shaped, You were.
Before breath became speech, You hovered.
Before creation had a name, You were naming.

You are the origin of meaning,
The source of sound,
The silence that sings.

I bow before the mystery of You,
Not just the Word spoken,
But the Word before speech.

Let me hear You in the stillness.
Let me know You beyond language.
Let me worship You in wonder.

Holy Spirit, help me hear the Word before words.
Teach me to listen with faith.
Amen.

CHAPTER 2

The Word That Speaks Creation

Genesis 1:3 KJV — "And God said, 'Let there be light,' and there was light."

This Scripture is the first recorded instance of divine speech, and it is pure creative power. No tools. No materials. No delay. God did not create light; He spoke it into existence. His Word does not need raw material; the Word creates it. His voice does not echo; it initiates. When He speaks, darkness flees, and light is. Creation responds to the Word. When God said, "Let there be light," He was not making a suggestion; He was unleashing reality. The Word did not merely describe creation, it became creation. Galaxies spun into being, oceans surged, molecules aligned, because the Word spoke.

That same Word still speaks. Jesus, the Word made flesh, continues to speak life into chaos, healing into brokenness, and purpose into wandering hearts. His voice calms storms, calls the dead to rise, and whispers peace into anxious souls. The Word that shaped the universe has not fallen silent; it is active, present, and personal, speaking over you.

Job 33:4 KJV — "The Spirit of God has made me; the breath of the Almighty gives me life."

Here, the focus shifts from cosmic creation to personal formation. The God who speaks worlds into existence is the same God who breathes life into you. You are not merely assembled; you are animated. The Spirit of God made you; the breath of the Almighty gave you life. It is not just poetic language, it is spiritual reality. Your very existence is a living testimony of God's creative breath. Every inhale is a reminder that you were spoken, shaped, and sustained by Him.

> *Psalm 119:105 KJV — "Thy word is a lamp unto my feet, and a light unto my path."*

Now the Word moves from shaping the universe to guiding your steps. The same voice that called stars into place also illuminates your daily walk.

- The Word doesn't just speak creation, it speaks direction.
- It lights the path when the way is unclear.
- It reveals the next step when the journey feels long.
- It doesn't always flood the whole road with light, but it always gives enough for the next faithful move.

> *John 1:3 KJV "All things were made by him; and without him was not anything made that was made."*

Jesus—the Word—is not simply present at creation; He is the agent through whom all things came into being. Nothing exists apart from Him. Every tree, every tide, every breath was made by Him—and that includes you. You are not accidental. You are handcrafted, intentionally brought forth by the Word who speaks life. Even the hidden parts of your story—your pain, your process, your becoming—are held within His creative, sustaining power.

Romans 4:17 KJV — "…*even God, who quickeneth the dead, and calleth those things which be not as though they were.*"

Here we see God's creative authority extending beyond nature into destiny, identity, and resurrection.

- God speaks to what is not as though it already is.
- He doesn't wait for evidence—He creates it.
- He doesn't need raw material—His Word is the material.

Our father of faith, Abraham, believed in a God who raises the dead and calls nations into being from a barren womb. That same God speaks over you today, calling purpose out of emptiness, life out of places that seem dead, and identity out of confusion.

Beloved, hold fast, the God who turned Abraham's impossibility into destiny is the same God who is shaping yours. Your present struggle is not the end, it is the soil where miracles take root, and your future will testify of His faithfulness. I am a living witness of His power and faithfulness.

―――――――――― *Reflection Point* ――――――――――

Before the world had form, the Word existed, eternal, alive, and divine. This Word did not merely comment on creation; it brought creation into being. Every mountain, molecule, and melody was born from divine utterance. The universe is not random, it is the echo of "God said."

Jesus, the Word made flesh, still speaks today. His voice creates healing from brokenness, peace from chaos, and purpose from confusion. When He speaks, things change—inside you and around you. You are not a random sound lost in the noise of the universe; you are a deliberate response to the Word. You were spoken into existence with intention, love, and power.

God's Word creates, and His Spirit breathes life into what is spoken. In His image, your words also carry weight. They can tear down or build up, wound or heal, distort or align with His creative heart. As you journey with this chapter, ask the Lord to speak light into your darkness and to teach you how to speak as He speaks, words that build, heal, and create according to His will.

Prayer: Speak, Lord—Create Again

Word of God,
You spoke light into darkness, form into void, and life into dust.
You are the breath behind every sunrise, the voice beneath every heartbeat.

Speak again, Lord—into me.
Where I am weary, speak strength.
Where I am broken, speak healing.
Where I am lost, speak direction.
Where I am silent, speak Your presence.

Let Your Word shape me as it shaped the stars.
Let Your voice call forth beauty from my chaos.
Let Your Spirit hover over my soul and birth something holy.

Jesus, Living Word,
I receive Your voice today—not as an echo, but as origin.
Create in me a clean heart.
Renew in me a steadfast spirit.
Speak, and I will become.
Amen.

CHAPTER 3

The Word Made Flesh

John 1:14 KJV — "And the Word was made flesh, and dwelt among us... full of grace and truth."

This verse reveals the miracle of the incarnation, the eternal, creative Word stepping into time, taking on flesh, and living among us. The Word did not remain distant; He became flesh—tangible, touchable, and vulnerable. He did not visit briefly; He dwelt among us as one of us. In Him, we beheld glory, not only in majesty but in mercy, not only in power but in intimate presence. He came full of grace and truth, not one or the other, but both held together in perfect balance. The same Word that spoke creation into being stepped into His own creation to redeem it.

Luke 1:35 KJV — "The Holy Ghost shall come upon thee... therefore... the Son of God."

Here we witness the holy mystery of how the Word became flesh, through the overshadowing of the Holy Spirit. The Word that once spoke galaxies into existence now enters a womb, not by human will or effort, but by divine initiative. The Holy Ghost comes upon Mary, and the power of the Highest wraps her in glory. What is conceived in her is the Son of God. Incarnation is beyond God coming near from the outside; it is God choosing to dwell within humanity. The Word becomes flesh not by force, but by overshadowing love, God with us, and, by His Spirit, God in us.

> *Philippians 2:6–8 KJV* — *"…He humbled himself, and became obedient unto death…"*

This passage shows the heart posture of the Word made flesh. The One who was in the form of God and equal with God did not cling to His glory. Instead, He humbled Himself, emptying Himself and taking the form of a servant. He entered human life not as a king demanding honor, but as a servant willing to suffer. He walked among us not to be praised, but to be pierced. This is divine humility: the Creator becoming a creature, the Speaker of stars submitting to death, the very Word who spoke life now willingly surrendering His own life for us.

> *Colossians 1:15–17 KJV* — *"…by him all things consist."*

Colossians declares the supremacy of Christ, the Word made flesh. He is the image of the invisible God, not a mere reflection but the complete revelation of God's nature. He is the firstborn of all creation, first in rank and authority over everything that exists. By Him all things were created—things seen and unseen, earthly and heavenly—and by Him all things hold together. The Christ who walked the dusty roads of earth is the same One who sustains galaxies and holds every heart in place. He is before all things, the reason for all things, and the One in whom everything finds its meaning and coherence—the very glue of existence.

Matthew 1:23 KJV — *"…Emmanuel… God with us."*

This verse gives us the name that captures the essence of the incarnation: Emmanuel—God with us. The Word did not merely echo from heaven; He entered the womb. He did not remain above us; He came to live among us. In Jesus, God's presence is not distant, abstract, or symbolic, but real and personal. The Creator becomes our companion. The Holy God takes on human flesh, sharing our sorrows, joys, burdens, and journeys. Emmanuel means that God is truly with us—near, present, and involved in the details of our lives.

Reflection Point

Jesus is the Word made flesh, conceived by the Spirit and revealed in human form. To look for the Word is, ultimately, to look for Christ—not only in theology and doctrine, but in His humanity, His humility, His obedience, and His love. In Him we see God's heart translated into a life we can watch, follow, and trust.

The incarnation assures us that God does not save us from a safe distance. He steps into our story, shares our weakness, and walks our roads. The One by whom all things consist is the same One who holds you together when life feels scattered or fragile. As you seek the Word, you are welcoming Emmanuel—God with you, God in you, and God for you.

Prayer: Overshadow Me, O God

Jesus,
Word made flesh, dwell in me by Your Spirit.
Let the Word take form in me,
Not just as thought, but as life.
Not just as a promise, but as a presence.

I yield to Your mystery.
I welcome Your movement.
I receive Your overshadowing.

Hold me together.
In my chaos, be my center.
In my questions, be my truth.
In my weakness, be my strength.

Let me live not just for You,
But by You,
Held together by Your Word.
Let the Son of God be glorified in me.
Amen.

CHAPTER 4

The Word in the Wilderness

Matthew 4:4 KJV — "But he answered and said, It is written, Man shall not live by bread alone, but by every word that proceedeth out of the mouth of God."

This verse is a powerful declaration of spiritual dependence, spoken by Jesus during His temptation in the wilderness. It affirms that the Word of God is not only creative but sustaining, not just the origin of life, but the nourishment of it. Bread feeds the body, but the Word feeds the soul. Jesus, the Living Word, reminds us that we are not sustained merely by what we consume, but by what God speaks. Every Word that proceeds from His mouth is life, strength in weakness, clarity in confusion, and victory in temptation.

Luke 4:1 KJV — "And Jesus, being full of the Holy Ghost, returned from Jordan, and was led by the Spirit into the wilderness."

This verse marks the beginning of Jesus' testing—not in weakness, but in Spirit-filled strength. It shows that the Word made flesh is not only powerful in proclamation, but obedient in preparation. Jesus enters the wilderness not by accident, but by the leading of the Spirit. He goes in not empty, but full of the Holy Ghost. Before miracles, before public ministry, the Word submits to silence, solitude, and struggle. This is a divine pattern: filled, then led, then tested, then proven.

> *Deuteronomy 8:3 KJV — "…that he might make thee know that man doth not live by bread only, but by every word that proceedeth out of the mouth of the Lord doth man live."*

Here we see that God uses wilderness seasons not to punish His people, but to teach them, especially the lesson that His Word is their true sustenance. He allowed Israel to experience hunger, not to harm them, but to humble them and reveal what was in their hearts. He fed them with manna, something unknown, unexpected, and undeserved, to show them that their lives were not sustained by bread alone, but by every word that proceeded from His mouth. This is wilderness wisdom: when bread runs out, the Word remains; when strength fails, the Word still feeds.

> *Psalm 119:11 KJV — "Thy word have I hid in mine heart, that I might not sin against thee."*

This verse shifts our focus from the outward wilderness to the inner life of the heart. The Word of God does not only shape galaxies, it guards souls. It is not meant to remain merely spoken, but stored; not just heard, but hidden; not only known, but carefully kept within. When the Word is treasured and buried deep in the heart, temptation begins to lose its grip, and sin its seduction. You do not walk only with information, but with inner armor. Hiding the Word in your heart is a spiritual strategy: you plant it so profoundly that it rises before sin does.

Isaiah 40:8 KJV — *"The grass withereth, the flower fadeth: but the word of our God shall stand forever."*

While creation is glorious, it is also temporary; grass withers. Flowers fade. Seasons change. Strength diminishes. But the Word of our God stands forever, unchanging, unshaken, eternal. The same Word that spoke light into being still speaks today. It is not subject to decay; instead, it is the source of renewal. In a world where everything else passes away, the Word remains a firm foundation and a faithful anchor.

Reflection Point

When everything around you change, the Word of God remains. When beauty fades, when strength fails, when time moves on, you can stand on what does not move. In the wilderness, Jesus was sustained by the Word and led by the Spirit. In our own deserts, whether of hardship, dryness, grief, or uncertainty, the Spirit still guides and the Word still feeds.

God may allow seasons where the "bread" you are used to runs out, where familiar supports, answers, or comforts are stripped away, not to destroy you, but to deepen your dependence on His voice. In those places, you learn that your life is upheld not by external provision alone, but by the living, proceeding Word from His mouth. His promises become your anchor. His truth becomes your compass. His voice becomes your lifeline.

Prayer: Feed Me with Your Word

Father,
I hunger for more than bread.
I thirst for more than comfort.
I need Your Word—fresh, living, sustaining.

Speak into my wilderness.
Feed me with truth.
Strengthen me with grace.
Let me live not by what I see,
But by what You say.

Let me not live by bread alone,
But by every word You speak.
Let me hunger for Your voice—
More than comfort, more than certainty.
Feed me with Your Word—
Fresh, daily, divine.
Amen.

CHAPTER 5

The Word That Heals

Luke 7:7 KJV — "…but say in a word, and my servant shall be healed."

This verse captures a remarkable encounter between Jesus and a Roman centurion. The centurion's servant was gravely ill, yet he did not insist that Jesus come physically to his house. Instead, he approached with deep humility and extraordinary faith, believing that a single spoken word from Jesus, even at a distance, was enough to bring healing. He did not feel worthy to approach Jesus directly or to have Jesus enter his home, but he understood that Jesus' Word carried divine authority. He believed that healing did not require physical touch, only a divine command. This response amazed Jesus, who said He had not found such great faith even in Israel. Here we see that faith transcends background, status, and proximity; it is ultimately about trusting the Word.

Romans 8:11 KJV — "…he that raised up Christ from the dead shall also quicken your mortal bodies by his Spirit that dwelleth in you."

This verse is a powerful promise of resurrection power, not only for the future, but for the present. The same Spirit who raised Jesus from the dead now lives in you. That Spirit does not merely comfort; He quickens. He brings life to what feels lifeless, strength to what feels weak, and healing to what feels broken. You are not abandoned in your frailty, nor powerless in your struggle. The resurrection power of Christ is active within you, working in your mortal body by His indwelling Spirit.

> *Psalm 107:20 KJV — "He sent his word, and healed them, and delivered them from their destructions."*

This verse shines as a radiant declaration of God's compassion and power. Healing and deliverance come not only through visible interventions, but through the Word itself. God does not need to send armies or vast visible forces to rescue; He sends His Word. That Word heals, rescues, and restores. Scripture is not mere information on a page, it is living, active, and transformative. When God sends His Word, He sends His power, His mercy, and His restoring grace.

> *Isaiah 53:5 KJV — "…with his stripes we are healed."*

This is one of the most profound prophetic declarations about Jesus Christ and His redemptive work. Jesus bore the punishment we deserved; His wounds were not random, but redemptive. His suffering purchased our peace within and peace with God. The lashes He endured became the pathway to our healing, physical, emotional, and spiritual. Healing is not something we earn or deserve; it is something we receive through the finished work of Christ. His pain became our restoration, His stripes our wholeness.

> *Mark 5:34 KJV — "Daughter, thy faith hath made thee whole; go in peace, and be whole of thy plague."*

This verse records Jesus' words to the woman with the issue of blood, who had suffered for twelve long years. She did not ask for public attention; she quietly reached out in faith to touch the hem of His garment. Jesus stopped and drew her out of the shadows, addressing her with tenderness and dignity: "Daughter." In that moment, He affirmed her identity and belonging. Her healing was not only physical; it was holistic. The affliction was gone, the shame was lifted, and her story was rewritten. Faith unlocked restoration, and Jesus sent her away not just healed, but whole. This shows us that healing is deeply personal, Jesus does not merely fix problems; He restores people wholesomely.

Reflection Point

Healing flows from the Word, empowered by the Spirit. The restoration God offers is not limited to the physical body; it reaches into the spiritual, emotional, and relational dimensions of our lives. Jesus' words heal hearts as well as bodies. The same Word that calmed storms, raised the dead, and silenced demons still speaks today, into trauma, fatigue, anxiety, and shame.

To receive healing is to trust that His Word carries authority over every sickness, wound, and broken place. It is believed that His stripes truly are our healing and that His Spirit is actively quickening our mortal bodies. When you look for the Word that heals, you are looking at Jesus, listening to His voice, trusting His promises, and opening every wound to His restoring power.

Prayer: Say the Word, Lord

Jesus,
You are the Word that heals.
You spoke, and light pierced darkness.
You whispered, and storms were stilled.
You commanded, and sickness fled.

I come not by merit, but by mercy.
Not by strength, but by surrender.
Like the centurion, I say:
"Lord, I am not worthy… but speak the Word."

Speak healing over my body—
Where pain lingers, let peace reign.
Where weakness dwells, let strength arise.
Where disease hides, let Your glory shine.

Speak healing over my mind—
Silence the lies.
Calm the storms.
Restore clarity.
Renew joy.

Speak healing over my heart—
Mend what is broken.
Revive what is weary.
Release what is bound.

Jesus, Word made flesh,
I receive Your healing Word.
Not as echo, but as authority.
Not as comfort alone, but as a transformation.
Say the Word, Lord—
And I shall be healed.
Amen.

CHAPTER 6

The Word in Us

> *Colossians 3:16 KJV — "Let the word of Christ dwell in you richly in all wisdom; teaching and admonishing one another in psalms and hymns and spiritual songs, singing with grace in your hearts to the Lord."*

This verse is an invitation to let the Word of Christ take up deep, abundant residence within us, not just in our minds, but in our spirits and emotions. When the Word dwells richly, it overflows in wisdom, shaping how we teach, encourage, and lovingly correct one another. It expresses itself in worship, psalms, hymns, and spiritual songs, and in hearts filled with grace toward the Lord. The Word in us becomes the music of our lives. It moves from text to song, from doctrine to devotion, from information to transformation.

> *John 14:26 KJV — "But the Comforter, which is the Holy Ghost... he shall teach you all things, and bring all things to your remembrance, whatsoever I have said unto you."*

Here, Jesus reveals the beautiful ministry of the Holy Spirit. The Spirit is not merely a vague presence; He is our Comforter, Teacher, and Reminder. He opens our understanding and brings the words of Christ back to our remembrance, not just on a mental level, but in a living, spiritual way. In moments of confusion, the Spirit recalls truth. In times of sorrow, He brings promises to mind. In seasons of decision, He guides us with the Word Jesus has already spoken.

> *Romans 10:8 KJV — "The word is nigh thee, even in thy mouth, and in thy heart: that is, the word of faith, which we preach."*

Paul reminds us that the Word of God is not unreachable. It is not locked away in heaven or buried in mystery. It is near, intimately close, right in your mouth and in your heart. This is the Word of faith, not only proclaimed but planted. God's Word is not reserved for the elite or the highly educated; it is accessible to the humble, the hungry, and the hurting. It is not just for scholars, it is for seekers.

When the Word is in your mouth, it begins to shape your speech, how you pray, how you declare, how you encourage others. When the Word is in your heart, it transforms your inner life, how you think, how you trust, how you endure. Faith is more than silent belief; it is spoken trust, the declaration that what God says is true even when circumstances argue otherwise. The Word of faith is not passive; it is active, alive, and powerful. To carry the Word in your mouth is to speak life. To carry the Word in your heart is to live by it.

> *James 1:22 KJV — "But be ye doers of the word, and not hearers only, deceiving your own selves."*

The Word in Us

James confronts us with a sobering reality: the Word is not meant only to be heard—it is meant to be lived. To listen without obeying is to step into self-deception, admiring truth without allowing it to shape our lives. Hearing alone is like building on sand; doing is building on rock. The Word is a seed, but it must be sown into daily choices. It is a lamp, but it must be carried into dark places. It is a sword, but it must be wielded in spiritual battles.

To be a doer of the Word is to let it shape your decisions, conversations, relationships, and responses to suffering. It means allowing Scripture to function as your strategy, your standard, and your strength. Hearing the Word fills the mind; doing the Word transforms the life. The Holy Spirit empowers us not only to understand what God says, but to walk it out, step by step, moment by moment, in grace and truth.

> *2 Timothy 3:16–17 KJV — "All scripture is given by inspiration of God… that the man of God may be perfect, thoroughly furnished unto all good works."*

Paul lifts our view of Scripture to its true height: it is God-breathed. Every verse carries the breath of God. Every passage holds purpose. The Word is not simply informative; it is profoundly transformative. It is profitable, not for our entertainment, but for our equipping. Through Scripture, God teaches us what is true, confronts what is false, corrects what is broken, and trains us to live in righteousness. This is Heaven's curriculum for spiritual maturity.

The Word does more than inspire; it prepares. It does more than comfort; it convicts and directs. It does more than decorate our minds with religious language; it furnishes our lives with everything needed for obedience and good works. To be "thoroughly furnished" is to be fully equipped, not empty-handed, not scrambling, but ready. Ready to serve, to love, to endure, to build, to bless. The Spirit breathes through Scripture to shape us into vessels of purpose. The Word is not only in us; it is actively working through us.

Reflection Point

The Word of God is not far away, sealed off in some unreachable realm. It is near, very near, placed by God in your mouth and in your heart. This is the Word of faith, not just preached from a pulpit, but planted in a person. To receive the Word is to receive Christ Himself. The Word is not just information; it is incarnation, Jesus' dwelling in us by the Spirit, renewing our minds, guiding our steps, and transforming our lives from within.

When the Word is in us, we begin to speak with grace because grace has already spoken to us. We walk in truth because Truth Himself walks within us. We endure trials because the Word strengthens us from the inside out. The Holy Spirit does more than remind us of verses; He activates them. He turns Scripture into direction, promises into power, and commands into compassion. The Word becomes our compass, our conviction, and our courage.

Yet, the Word must be lived. James warns that hearing without doing leads to self-deception. The Word is not a mirror we glance at and then forget; it is a map we follow. Through Scripture, God thoroughly equips us for every good work, furnishing us with wisdom, humility, and holy boldness. When the Word truly dwells in us, we become living epistles, letters of Christ, written not with ink, but with the Spirit of the living God. We live not merely informed, but transformed.

Prayer: Living Word

Living Word,
You are not far—you are near.
You dwell in my heart.
You stir in my spirit.
You speak through Scripture, and You whisper through silence.

Let Your Word shape my speech.
Let Your truth guide my choices.
Let Your Spirit activate what You've planted in me.

Make me not just a hearer, but a doer.
Not just a student, but a servant.
Not just informed, but transformed.

Let Your Word live in me—
As seed, as sword, as song.
Let me carry Your voice into every room I enter.
Let me become a vessel of Your Word—
Faithful, fruitful, and filled with grace.
Amen.

Personal Notes

CHAPTER 7

The Word That Waits

1 Kings 19:12 KJV — "And after the earthquake a fire; but the Lord was not in the fire: and after the fire a still small voice."

God's voice is not always found in the dramatic. Elijah had just witnessed a great wind, an earthquake, and a fire—but the Lord was not in any of them. Then came a still small voice: gentle, quiet, and holy. This verse reminds us that the Word often comes in whispers, not shouts; in silence, not spectacle; in stillness, not storm. The Word that waits is also the Word that whispers. It does not compete with noise; it invites us into quiet. It does not demand attention; it draws us into intimacy. The still small voice is the Spirit's way of saying, "I am near. Listen deeper." To hear the whisper, we must quiet our hearts, turn down the volume of fear, distraction, and urgency. The whisper is not weak—it is sacred. It is the voice of a God who chooses intimacy over intimidation.

Habakkuk 2:3 KJV — "For the vision is yet for an appointed time… though it tarry, wait for it; because it will surely come…"

God's Word is never rushed. It moves according to divine timing, not human urgency. The vision—the Word, the promise, the prophecy—is for an appointed time. It may seem delayed, but it is not denied. The Word waits until the soil is ready, the heart is prepared, and the season is ripe. It speaks at the end, not with hesitation, but with truth. It does not lie, and it does not fail. Waiting is not weakness; it is worship. To wait is to trust the Author of time. To wait is to believe that what God has spoken will come to pass. Even when the answer feels slow, the Word is sure. Even when the vision tarries, it is still moving—quietly, faithfully, toward fulfilment.

> *Psalm 130:5 KJV — "I wait for the Lord, my soul doth wait, and in his word do I hope."*

Waiting is not passive; it is a spiritual posture. The psalmist is not merely waiting for an outcome or an answer—he is waiting for the Lord Himself. And while he waits, he anchors his hope in the Word. To wait for the Lord is to trust His presence more than His pace. To hope in His Word is to believe that every promise is alive, even in silence. The Word that waits is also the Word that sustains. It holds us steady when emotions waver, when outcomes are delayed, and when prayers seem unanswered. God's Word is not just a past declaration; it is a present companion, walking with us through the night and whispering, "I am faithful. I am near. I will come."

> *Romans 8:26 KJV — "…the Spirit itself maketh intercession for us with groanings which cannot be uttered."*

The Word That Waits

There are moments when words fail—when pain runs too deep, confusion too thick, and silence too heavy. In those moments, the Spirit steps in. He does not simply observe our weakness; He helps. He does not merely hear our silence; He translates it. The Word that waits is also the Word that intercedes. When we do not know what to pray, the Spirit prays through us. When our voice trembles, His groaning rises. When our language falters, His presence speaks. This is divine intimacy—God not only listening, but joining our prayer. The Spirit does not require eloquence; He responds to honesty. He does not wait for perfect words; He moves through surrendered hearts. To carry the Word in us is to have the Spirit who prays for us. Even in weakness, we are never voiceless. Even in silence, we are never alone.

Isaiah 40:31 KJV — "But they that wait upon the Lord shall renew their strength…"

Waiting on the Lord is not passive; it is active and potent. Isaiah reveals a divine exchange:

- **When we wait, God renews**
- **When we pause, He empowers**
- **When we trust, He lifts**

The Word that waits is also the Word that strengthens. It does not only speak comfort; it breathes courage. It does not merely promise rest; it delivers renewal. To wait upon the Lord is to lean into His timing, His wisdom, and His Spirit—to surrender our pace and receive His power. The eagle does not exhaust itself by constant flapping; it learns to soar on the wind.

In the same way, strength is not found in striving but in surrender. In this rhythm of grace, we mount up and rise above what once held us down, we run toward purpose without weariness, and we walk through the long journey without fainting. The Word in us waits, renews, and lifts, teaching us that strength is not earned—it is received.

> *Lamentations 3:26 KJV — "It is good that a man should both hope and quietly wait for the salvation of the Lord."*

In a world of urgency and noise, this verse offers a gentle, countercultural truth: waiting can be good. Not just tolerable, but spiritually fruitful. Salvation often comes not in haste, but in holy stillness. To quietly wait is to trust God's timing more than our own deadlines. To hope while waiting is to anchor the soul in promise rather than in visible proof. The Word that waits is not idle; it is active in the unseen. It is working in silence, preparing in stillness, and maturing in mystery. God's salvation is worth the wait, and the waiting itself becomes sacred when filled with hope.

> *Psalm 46:10 KJV — "Be still, and know that I am God…"*

Stillness is not inactivity; it is intimacy. This verse invites us into a sacred pause in which knowing God begins not with striving but with surrender. To be still is to stop fighting battles that belong to God, to quiet the inner noise, and to listen for His whisper. It is to recognize that God is sovereign, present, and exalted—

whether we see it or not. The Word that waits also speaks in stillness. It does not shout to compete with the chaos; it settles in to reveal the truth. In stillness, we do not simply hear about God—we come to know Him. This is the posture of trust, the rhythm of reverence, and the place where the Word becomes more than instruction—it becomes encounter.

Reflection Point

The Word of God is not always immediate. It does not bow to our timelines or hurry to match our urgency. It waits—because it is wise, intentional, and eternal. From Habakkuk's vision to Isaiah's promise of renewed strength, Scripture teaches that waiting is not weakness; it is worship. The Word waits in silence, in stillness, in seasons of preparation. It waits in the womb before incarnation, in the wilderness before ministry, and in the tomb before resurrection. In the silence, the Spirit groans. In the stillness, trust grows. The Word waits to be revealed at the right time, in the right way. God's Word is not always loud; it often waits in mystery. Our task is to learn to listen.

Prayer: Lord of Time and Truth

Lord of Time and Truth,
You speak with power, and You wait with purpose.
Your Word does not rush—it ripens.
It does not falter—it fulfills.

I believe what You have spoken will come to pass.
Teach me to wait with faith.
To trust Your silence as much as Your speech.
Let me rest in Your promises, even when the answer tarries.

In the stillness, let me hear Your whisper.
In the delay, let me feel Your presence.
In the longing, let me hold fast to Your Word.

You are not slow—you are sovereign.
You are not absent—you are preparing.
You are not silent—you are speaking in ways I must learn to hear.

So I wait, Lord—
Not with weariness, but with worship.
Not with fear, but with faith.
Not with doubt, but with deep hope.

Let Your Word be my anchor,
My hope,
My quiet confidence.

Let Your Word live in me,
Grow in me,
And come forth in Your perfect time.

And I will wait for it.
Amen.

CHAPTER 8

The Word That Sends

Isaiah 6:8 KJV — "Also I heard the voice of the Lord, saying, Whom shall I send, and who will go for us? Then said I, Here am I; send me."

Isaiah 6:8 captures a sacred moment of calling. The prophet, freshly cleansed and humbled in the presence of God, hears a question reverberating through the throne room: "Whom shall I send, and who will go for us?" It is not forced upon him; it is an invitation, not a command, a call, not a coercion. Isaiah responds with the words that mark every willing servant: "Here am I; send me." The Word that waits also sends. It waits for readiness, for surrender, for hearts that say yes. God does not send the perfect, but the purified; not the self-qualified, but the ones He has called. To say "send me" is to step into divine purpose, to carry the Word into the world not only in speech, but in service. It is to become a vessel of God's voice, a messenger of mercy, a bearer of truth. The Spirit still asks, "Who will go for us?" and the Word in us still answers, "Here am I."

Acts 13:2 KJV — "As they ministered to the Lord, and fasted, the Holy Ghost said, separate me Barnabas and Saul for the work whereunto I have called them."

In the quiet rhythm of worship and fasting, the Holy Spirit speaks. Acts 13:2 reveals a moment of divine clarity born not of human strategy but of surrender. As the believers ministered to the Lord and fasted, the Word came, not merely to comfort, but to commission. The Word that waits also calls. It speaks in consecrated spaces and moves through yielded hearts. Barnabas and Saul were not set apart because they were loud or impressive; they were chosen because they were ready and responsive. The Spirit did not interrupt their plans so much as reveal His. In that moment, ministry became mission, and devotion became deployment. To minister to the Lord is to make room for His voice. To fast is to clear space for His direction. To be separated is to be set apart, not for isolation, but for impact. The Word in us does not only dwell; it deploys.

Matthew 28:19–20 KJV — "Go ye therefore, and teach all nations… I am with you always, even unto the end of the world. Amen."

This Scripture captures the Great Commission: the heartbeat of mission and the echo of Christ's final earthly instruction. The Word does not simply abide in us; it sends us out. We are told to go, not only geographically, but spiritually and relationally, stepping beyond comfort into calling. We are to teach all nations, because the Word is for everyone. We baptize in the Name of the Father, the Son, and the Holy Ghost, welcoming people into a new identity and family. We teach them to observe all that Jesus commanded, because the Word shapes life, not only belief. And we go with this assurance: "I am with you always." The Word that sends also stays. Christ goes with us into classrooms and kitchens, into prisons and pulpits, into crowded rooms and quiet conversations. His presence is the power behind the commission.

> *Jeremiah 1:7 KJV — "Say not, I am a child: for thou shalt go to all that I shall send thee…"*

Jeremiah stood before God, hesitating, protesting, "I am a child." But the Lord answered not with indulgence of his excuses, but with commissioning. He did not affirm Jeremiah's insecurity; He corrected it. When God sends, He equips. When He calls, He empowers. God's "Say not" silences self-doubt. His "thou shalt go" directs the journey. His "thou shalt speak" provides the message. This is the rhythm of divine calling: it is not determined by age, status, or eloquence, but by surrender. Our weakness does not limit the Word in us; it is activated by our willingness. To be sent by God is to go where He leads, speak what He commands, and trust that His presence goes before us.

> *John 20:21 KJV — "Peace be unto you: as my Father hath sent me, even so send I you."*

Here, the risen Christ speaks to His disciples—not from a position of theory, but from a place marked by pierced hands and fulfilled promises.

- His first gift is peace: "Peace be unto you."
- His second gift is purpose: "As my Father hath sent me, even so send I you."

The Word that came into the world now commissions others to go in His name. Jesus was sent in humility, in power, and in love, and He sends us the same way. We are sent in peace, not driven by fear but filled with His presence. We are sent with authority, not our own, but His. We are sent with a mission: to carry the Word, embody grace, and reveal truth. The Word that sends does so gently, but with fire. It does not push; it empowers. It does not abandon; it accompanies. To be sent by Jesus is to walk in the echo of His own journey, bearing light, speaking life, and living love wherever we go.

Reflection Point

The Word of God does not only comfort; it commissions. It does not only dwell; it deploys. From Isaiah's trembling "Here am I" to Jesus' commanding "Go ye therefore," Scripture reveals a consistent pattern: those who encounter the Word are sent by it. The Spirit speaks the sending Word, and we are invited into partnership with God's mission in the world. We do not go in our own strength, wisdom, or authority; we go in His. We are not only carriers of information, but bearers of presence. The Word in us becomes the Word through us, as we step into assignments big and small, loving neighbors, preaching Christ, serving the least, and shining light in dark places.

We are commissioned not only by command, but by presence. The One who sends us also goes with us. The Word that called us is the same Word that sustains us on the journey. We are messengers of grace, ambassadors of reconciliation, and witnesses of a Kingdom that cannot be shaken. To look for the Word is not only to listen; it is to answer, "Here am I. Send me."

Prayer: Lord of the Harvest

Lord of the harvest,
You speak with purpose, and You send with power.
Your Word does not stay idle—it moves through us.
It finds the willing, the surrendered, the listening.

Here am I, Lord—send me.

Send me not in my strength, but in Yours.
Send me not with my words, but with Your truth.
Send me not alone, but with Your Spirit.

Let me carry Your Word with reverence,
Speak it with boldness,
Live it with grace.

Where You lead, I will follow.
Where You speak, I will echo.
Where You send, I will go.

Silence my excuses.
Strengthen my steps.
Sanctify my mission.

Let Your Word in me become a light for others.
Let Your sending becomes my surrender.
Let Your presence goes before me,
And Your glory be my aim.

Here I am, Lord. Send me with Your Word.
Amen.

CHAPTER 9

The Word and the Spirit (Divine Partnership)

2 Corinthians 3:6 KJV — "Who also hath made us able ministers of the New Testament; not of the letter, but of the spirit: for the letter killeth, but the spirit giveth life."

This verse draws a powerful contrast between law and Spirit—between mere words on a page and the living presence of God. Paul reminds us that we are not just messengers of doctrine; we are ministers of life. The Word that sends us is not rigid; it is radiant. It is not cold ink; it is burning breath. "Not of the letter…" reminds us that the law alone cannot save; it can reveal our condition, but it cannot redeem us. "But of the spirit…" shows that the Spirit animates the Word, turning command into communion and truth into transformation. "The letter killeth…" warns that even Spirit animates the Word, turning command into communion and truth into transformation. "The letter killeth…" warns that even Scripture, handled without the Spirit, can become a weapon that wounds instead of heals. "The spirit giveth life" declares that, with the Spirit, the Word becomes a wellspring—full of grace, power, and renewal. The Word that sends must be carried in the Spirit —spoken with grace, lived with humility, and shared with love. We are proclaimers: we are partakers of a living covenant.

John 6:63 KJV — *"It is the spirit that quickeneth; the flesh profiteth nothing: the words that I speak unto you, they are spirit, and they are life."*

Jesus speaks with piercing clarity: it is the Spirit who gives life; the flesh, on its own, can achieve nothing of eternal value. His words are not mere syllables or ideas; they are spirit and life—charged with divine energy and grace. The Spirit quickens, awakening what is dead, reviving what is weary, and empowering what is weak. Human effort without the Spirit "profiteth nothing," no matter how sincere or disciplined. But the words Christ speaks carry the very life of God. They do not just teach; they touch. They do not just instruct; they infuse. The Word that sends must be Spirit-filled, the Word that waits must be Spirit-led, and the Word that lives in us must be Spirit-breathed. To carry the Word is to carry life itself.

Ephesians 6:17 KJV — *"And take the helmet of salvation, and the sword of the Spirit, which is the word of God."*

In Paul's description of the armor of God, the Word is not only protection; it is power. The helmet of salvation covers our thoughts with assurance, identity, and hope. It reminds us that we are saved, secure, and sealed in Christ, deflecting lies, doubts, and despair. The sword of the Spirit, "which is the word of God," is not forged by human hands, but by the breath of God. It is living, active, and sharp. The Word that sends also defends; the Word that waits also wars; the Word that lives in us also speaks through us. To carry the Word is to be equipped for battle, not with fear but with faith, not in the strength of the flesh but in the power of the Spirit. Let the Word guard your mind and guide your steps. Let it shape your thoughts and sharpen your witness.

1. The Spirit Authored the Word

2 Timothy 3:16 KJV — "All scripture is given by inspiration of God…"

The Word of God is not merely ink on paper; the Spirit breathes it. The Holy Spirit inspired prophets, apostles, and writers to record divine truth. Without the Spirit, Scripture would be just a historical record. With Him, it becomes a living revelation. Every word is "inspired," God-breathed, so every verse carries divine breath and holy intent. The Word is profitable for doctrine, teaching us what is true. It is profitable for reproof and correction, confronting what is false and restoring what is broken. It is profitable for instruction in righteousness, training us to walk rightly and live holy.

The Scripture affirms that the Word is a living organism. It is not static; it is surgical. It cuts and heals, it exposes and mends, it guides and grows us. It forms the heart of the messenger before it flows from the mouth. It transforms the soul before it touches the world.

- To carry the Word is to be shaped by it.
- To speak the Word is to surrender to its authority.
- To live the Word is to reflect its righteousness.

Prayer:

Holy Spirit,
Breathe on the Word in me.
Let it come alive.
Confirm it with power,
Enforce it with truth,
Make it fruitful in my life.
Let me never separate Your voice from Your Word.
Amen.

2. The Spirit Illuminates the Word

John 16:13 KJV — "He will guide you into all truth…"

The Holy Spirit is the divine interpreter of Scripture. He opens our eyes to understand, convicts our hearts to respond, and reveals Christ through the Word. Without the Spirit, we read with intellect alone; with Him, we read with revelation. The Spirit does not replace the Word; He illuminates it. He turns ink into fire, doctrine into encounter, and memory into moment-by-moment revelation. When the Spirit moves, a verse becomes a voice, a promise becomes a path, and a command becomes a calling. He teaches us not only what the Word says, but what it means for us today, in our wilderness, in our healing, in our becoming. To read without the Spirit is to see letters; to read with the Spirit is to hear life.

Prayer:

Holy Spirit,

Illuminate the Word.
Let me not just read but receive.
Let me not just study but surrender.
Let me not just memorize but be transformed.
Amen.

3. The Spirit Confirms the Word

> *Hebrews 2:4 KJV — "God also bearing them witness… with signs and wonders…"*

When the Word is preached or declared, the Spirit confirms it with power. This confirmation may come through healing, deep conviction, prophetic insight, answered prayer, or supernatural peace. God bears witness to His message through signs, wonders, miracles, and gifts of the Holy Ghost, distributed according to His will. It is divine endorsement, the invisible Word made visible through supernatural acts. A healing becomes a testimony. A miracle becomes a message. A spiritual gift becomes a glimpse of God's glory. The Spirit does not perform for spectacle; He confirms for faith. Every sign is a signature. Every wonder is a whisper. Every gift is a grace pointing back to the faithfulness of the Word.

Prayer:
Lord,
Let Your Word be confirmed in me.
Let signs follow my surrender.
Let wonders awaken my worship.
Let gifts flow from Your Spirit.
Let my life be a living witness that Your Word is true, powerful, and alive. Amen.

4. The Spirit Enforces the Word

> *Jeremiah 23:29 KJV — "Is not my word like as a fire… and like a hammer…?"*

God's Word is not passive; it is power. Like fire, it purifies, consuming what cannot remain—falsehood, pride, and impurity. Like a hammer, it shatters what stands in the way—hardened hearts, stubborn habits, and spiritual strongholds. The Word of God both burns and breaks: it burns away what is unholy and breaks open what is unyielding. This is not sentimental poetry; it is divine force. The Word confronts, convicts, and clears the path for truth. It is not always comfortable, but it is always necessary.

> *Ephesians 6:17 KJV — "And take the helmet of salvation, and the sword of the Spirit, which is the word of God."*

The Word is not only a guide; it is a weapon. The helmet of salvation guards your mind, identity, and hope, reminding you that you are rescued, redeemed, and secure in Christ. The sword of the Spirit is the Word wielded by the Spirit Himself—sharp, precise, and alive. It cuts through confusion, exposes deception, and defends truth. This is not passive faith; it is active warfare. The Spirit does not leave us defenseless; He equips us with truth that both protects and prevails.

Prayer:

Holy Spirit,
Wield Your Word within me.
Guard my mind with the helmet of salvation.
Train my heart to fight with truth.
Let Your Word be both my defense and my declaration.
Let me stand and not in fear, but in faith.
Clothed in salvation.
Armed with the sword.
Ready for battle.
Amen.

5. The Spirit Makes the Word Fruitful

> Luke 8:11 KJV — "Now the parable is this: The seed is the word of God."

The Word of God is not static; it is a seed. Jesus reveals that His teachings are meant to be planted, nurtured, and multiplied. The

Word carries life, but its fruitfulness depends on the soil of the heart. A seed may appear small and insignificant, yet it holds the blueprint of transformation. It waits for surrender, thrives in faith, and grows through obedience. The Word is not only spoken; it is sown. It is meant to take root, break through hard ground, and bear fruit in character, love, and legacy.

Prayer:
Lord,
Let Your Word be planted deep in me.
Break up the hardness.
Clear away the clutter.
Let Your truth take root.
Let it grow into wisdom, love, and legacy.
Make my life fertile ground for Your Word.
Amen.

> 2 Corinthians 3:6 KJV — *"…not of the letter, but of the spirit: for the letter killeth, but the spirit giveth life."*

The Word of God is sacred, but without the Spirit, it can become sterile, even deadly. Paul draws a sharp contrast: the letter defines, but the Spirit delivers; the letter instructs, but the Spirit indwells. The Word is a seed, but the Spirit is the rain. He nurtures what is planted, brings conviction, and causes growth. Without the Spirit, the Word may be heard but not truly received. With Him, it bears fruit in transformed lives. We are not called to be cold carriers of commandments, but living ministers of the new covenant, animated by grace, guided by truth, and empowered by the Spirit.

Prayer:

Holy Spirit,
Breathe life into the Word I carry.
Let me not minister by letter alone,
But by Your living presence.
Let Your Word in me be fire, not formula.
Let it heal, not harm.
Let it lift, not limit.
Make me a vessel of life,
Not just of knowledge, but of Spirit.
Amen.

The Word and the Spirit are inseparable. The Spirit authors the Word, illuminates it, confirms it, enforces it, and makes it fruitful. Without the Spirit, the Word can become law, true, but lifeless in our hands. With the Spirit, it becomes life, truth applied, power released, grace revealed. To walk in the Word is to walk in the Spirit. The Spirit never contradicts the Word; He confirms it, empowers it, and applies it to hearts and circumstances.

Reflection Point

When we read Scripture, we must invite the Spirit to breathe on it. When we speak Scripture, we must trust the Spirit to enforce it. When we live Scripture, we must rely on the Spirit to sustain it. The Christian life is not merely a commitment to a text, but a covenant with a Person, the Living Word, made real in us by the Holy Spirit. The Word is our foundation; the Spirit is our fuel. Together, they form a divine partnership that shapes us into the image of Christ.

Prayer: Divine Partnership

Holy Father,
You spoke, and the worlds were formed.
You breathed, and life began.
Your Word is eternal truth unshaken.
Your Spirit is living power unbound.

Together, they move in perfect unity:
- *The Word declares,*
- *The Spirit activates.*
- *The Word instructs,*
- *The Spirit empowers.*
- *The Word reveals,*
- *The Spirit illuminates.*

Lord, I welcome this divine partnership in me.
Let Your Word dwell richly in my heart—
Not as ink, but as fire.
Not as law, but as life.

Let Your Spirit breathe upon it—
Making it alive, sharp, and fruitful.
Teach me to listen with spiritual ears,
To speak with Spirit-led wisdom,
To walk in Word-shaped obedience.

Where I am dry, pour out Your Spirit.
Where I am weary, let both Word and Spirit renew me.
May I never separate what You have joined.

Let Your Word be my foundation.
Let Your Spirit be my fuel.
Together, let them shape me into Your image.

In Jesus' name,
Amen.

SECTION TWO

From Quadriplegia to Anastasia

In "*Look for the Word*," we began with a simple yet profound invitation: to seek the voice of God in Scripture, in silence, and in the ordinary rhythms of life. That journey awakened us to the presence of the Word, not just as text, but as Person, Spirit, and Breath of life.

This companion section continues that journey. It leads us from **Quadriplegia,** a state where movement ends and listening begins, signifying stillness and inner awakening, to **Anastasia,** the Greek word for resurrection, where identity is restored and purpose renewed.

This transition is not instant, but gradual. We move from the paralysis of Quadriplegia, marked by silence and reflection, into the awakening and praise represented by Anastasia. Quadriplegia, in this context, is more than a medical diagnosis; it becomes a metaphor. It describes a paralysis we all encounter, fear, grief, despair, exhaustion. In this place, movement halts and stillness emerges, symbolizing the moment before transformation and the opening of a door to renewal.

Into that stillness, grace speaks.

> 2 Corinthians 12:9 — "*My grace is sufficient for you, for my power is made perfect in weakness.*"

Quadriplegia is not a barrier; it is a threshold. It reveals the limits of human strength and our deep need for divine grace. Our weakness is not the end of the story—it is the place where God's power is made perfect.

John 11:25 — "I am the resurrection and the life."

Resurrection is not only a future event at the end of time; it is also a present reality. Courage in the face of fear, hope in the midst of despair, and even joy in the middle of pain are all expressions of resurrection life. Anastasia is not an escape from suffering, but a transformation within it—a rising into newness of life, even while scars remain.

Anastasia, then, is not simply the endpoint of a journey out of stillness; it is a rhythm—the heartbeat of resurrection pulsing through every awakening, every "yes" to grace, every step taken in faith after a season of paralysis. Through the lens of Christian faith, this arc mirrors the Gospel itself:

- **The Cross**: where suffering is not abandoned but embraced
- **The Tomb**: where silence becomes sacred
- **The Resurrection**: where the Word speaks life again

This section is more than a devotional—it is a call to rise, again and again. A call to rise from fear, from despair, from the quiet paralysis of the soul.

So come—look again.
The Word is waiting.

Personal Notes

CHAPTER 10

Quadriplegia
The Stillness Where the Word Whispers

Quadriplegia is more than a physical condition. In this chapter, it becomes a picture of sacred stillness. Movement stops, but meaning deepens. When the body is confined and the usual rhythms of life are interrupted, the presence of God can feel more real. The spirit can find a deeper place of communion. This chapter is not primarily about limitation; it is about listening. The focus shifts away from striving and achievement to the whisper of holy presence. It does not chase what feels impossible. Instead, it pays attention to what God reveals in quietness.

Here, the Word of God does not shout. It whispers. It speaks in the hush of pain, in the pause of healing, in the breath between tears. It does not need volume to be heard. It needs surrender. Quadriplegia becomes a kind of sanctuary, a metaphorical altar where immobility is transformed into receptive stillness, inviting a sacred encounter. It is a holy hush where the Spirit hovers, a stillness where Scripture breathes, a place where the Word waits to be received, not with hands, but with the heart.

In this chapter, we do not rush. We rest. We do not strive. We listen. We do not try to escape the stillness. We embrace it. Because here, in the quiet, the Word whispers, and we are changed.

Psalm 46:10 — KJV—"Be still, and know that I am God..."

Stillness is not weakness. It is worship. In Psalm 46:10, God invites us to stop striving, lay down our defenses, and know. Not to analyze, perform, or prove, but to know that He is God. For one living with quadriplegia, this verse becomes a sanctuary. When you cannot move, knowing becomes everything. Where motion ends, revelation can begin. God does not ask for your strength. He asks for your surrender:

- To be still is to trust
- To be still is to listen
- To be still is to receive

In the stillness, the Word whispers.
In the quiet, the Spirit moves.
In the pause, God is present.

Prayer: In the Stillness, I Know

Lord,
Teach me to be still,
Not just in body, but in soul.
Let my stillness become a sanctuary.
Let my silence become surrender.

In the absence of motion,
Let Your presence be magnified.
In the quiet of my condition,
Let Your Word speak louder than pain.

I do not need to move to know You.
I do not need to strive to hear You.
I only need to be still,
And know.

You are God.
You are near.
You are enough.
Amen.

> *2 Corinthians 12:9 KJV— "And he said unto me, My grace is sufficient for thee, for my strength is made perfect in weakness…"*

God does not remove every thorn. Instead, He reveals His grace through it. In this verse, Paul opens a divine paradox. Weakness does not block the power of God. It becomes the very place where His power begins to work. When human strength runs out, grace steps forward. Quadriplegia may feel like a severe limitation, but in the Spirit, it becomes an invitation. It invites you to rely on God more deeply, to receive from Him more fully, and to rest in Him more completely.

- It is an invitation to rely.
- It is an invitation to receive.
- It is an invitation to rest.

The strength of God cannot be earned. It is always a gift. It comes not in the absence of weakness, but in the midst of it. Your story is not ultimately about what you cannot do. It is about what God chooses to do in you and through you, even now.

Prayer: Your Grace Is Enough

Lord,
I bring my weakness to You.
Not to hide it, but to offer it.
Not to be ashamed, but to be transformed.

You do not ask me to be strong.
You ask me to surrender.
You do not wait for my healing to begin.
You begin healing in my waiting.

Let Your grace be enough for me.
Enough when I cannot move.
Enough when I cannot speak.
Enough when I feel forgotten.

Let Your strength be made perfect here,
In the stillness, in the silence, in the suffering.
Let Your Word rise in me,
Not as noise, but as knowing.
Not as a command, but as comfort.

I do not need to prove anything.
I only need to receive everything.
Your grace is sufficient.
Your power is present.
Your love is relentless.

So, I rest,
Not in my ability,
But in Yours.
Amen.

Job 23:10 KJV — "But he knoweth the way that I take: when he hath tried me, I shall come forth as gold."

Job's declaration is not one of certainty in circumstance, but of confidence in God's character. Amid suffering, silence, and confusion, Job affirms that God knows his path. Even when the way is unclear, the outcome is secure: refinement, not ruin.

Quadriplegia may feel like a trial, but it is also a refining fire. God does not abandon in affliction; He purifies through it. He sees the way you take, even when you cannot walk it. He knows your heart, even when your body cannot express it.

- You are not lost in the trial.
- You are being shaped in it.
- You are not forgotten in the fire.
- You are becoming gold.

Prayer: Refine Me in the Fire

Lord,
You know the way I take—
Even when I cannot take a single step.
You see me in the fire, not as broken, but as becoming.

Let this trial not be wasted.
Let this suffering not be silent.
Let this stillness be sacred.

Refine me, not with wrath, but with mercy.
Shape me, not with shame, but with grace.

Let me come forth—
Not bitter, but beautiful.
Not hardened, but holy.

You are the Refiner.
You are the Watcher of my path.
You are the Whisper in my stillness.

So I trust You—
Not because I understand,
But because You are faithful.

Make me gold, Lord.
Not for my glory,
But for Yours.
Amen.

―――― *Reflection Point* ――――

1. Stillness Is Not Absence—It Is Invitation

Quadriplegia may silence the body, but it amplifies the soul's capacity to listen. In the absence of movement, the presence of God becomes more tangible. Stillness is not a void—it is a sanctuary where the Word whispers.

> *"Be still and know…" is not a command to do nothing—it is a call to recognize everything.*

2. God Speaks in Whispers, Not Always in Thunder

Elijah did not hear God in the wind, earthquake, or fire—but in a gentle whisper. In suffering, God's voice often comes softly, intimately, personally. The whisper is not weakness—it is closeness. In the quiet of limitation, God's Word becomes audible. In the hush of pain, His truth becomes undeniable.

3. Weakness Is a Canvas for Grace

Paul's thorn did not disqualify him—it qualified him for deeper revelation. Quadriplegia may feel like confinement, but it is also consecration. God's power is not hindered by weakness—it is highlighted through it. The Word whispers: "My grace is sufficient." Not despite your weakness—but through it.

4. The Spirit Intercedes When Words Fail

When the body cannot speak, the Spirit does.
When prayers are wordless, the Spirit groans.
You are not voiceless—you are Spirit-filled.
The Word still moves, even when you cannot.
Stillness is not silence—it is Spirit-led surrender.

5. Rest Is Not Defeat—It Is Dependence

Stillness is not surrender to suffering—it is surrender to God.
In the quiet, He heals.
In the pause, He speaks.
In the waiting, He moves.

> *Psalm 62:1 KJV— "Truly my soul waiteth upon God: from him cometh my salvation."*

Prayer: In the Stillness, Speak

Lord God,
In the stillness where limbs do not move, Let Your Word move freely.
In the quiet where pain lingers, Let Your whisper bring peace.

You are not absent in suffering—You are present in power.
You do not wait for strength to speak—You speak into weakness with grace.

When my body cannot rise,
Let my spirit soar to meet You.
When my voice cannot cry out,
Let Your Spirit groan on my behalf.

You are the Word that speaks in silence,
The breath that fills empty lungs,
The whisper that calms the storm within.

Let me hear You in the hush of limitation.
Let me receive You in the pause of healing.
Let me know You—not by motion, but by presence.

You do not need movement to minister.
You are the Word that waits. The Word that heals.
The Word that calls me by name.

Holy Spirit,
Hover over my stillness.
Interpret my silence.
Translate my tears.
Let Your Word find me here—In the place where limbs fail,
But faith listens.

Jesus,
Speak again.
Not to my body first, but to my soul.
Let Your Word be my breath,
My compass,
My resurrection.
Amen.

CHAPTER 11

Transformation
The Word as Healing and Identity

The Word of God does not merely inform; it transforms. It does not only speak to the mind; it ministers to the soul. It does not simply comfort; it reclaims. In the valley, the Word speaks life, calling us by name and reminding us that we are not forgotten. Transformation begins not with effort, but with revelation. In the aftermath of suffering, in the stillness of quadriplegia, the metaphor becomes medicine. The Word shifts from message to healing, its movement within us echoing resurrection itself.

Healing begins not with movement, but with meaning. Not with physical restoration, but with spiritual revelation. The Word enters the broken places, not to shame them, but to shape them. This is where identity is reborn. Not in what the world says, but in what God speaks. Not in what was lost, but in what is found in Christ.

The Word heals by naming. It calls you beloved. It calls you chosen. It calls you whole. You are not defined by diagnosis, limitation, or silence. You are defined by the Word that formed you, the Word that found you, and the Word that now transforms you. In this chapter, we look for the Word that restores. We receive the Word that redefines. We rise with the Word that resurrects.

Psalm 107:20 KJV — "He sent his word, and healed them, and delivered them from their destructions."

God does not wait for us to arrive at healing. He sends His Word to meet us in our brokenness. His Word is not bound by distance, diagnosis, or despair. It travels. It penetrates. It restores. When destruction surrounds us, whether through physical affliction, emotional collapse, or spiritual confusion, God's Word becomes a lifeline. It not only soothes symptoms. It rewrites outcomes.

Healing is not always the absence of pain. It is often the presence of purpose. The Word of God enters our story not to erase it, but to redeem it. He sends His Word like a messenger of mercy, carrying healing, identity, and deliverance. You are not forgotten. You are not forsaken. You are being healed by the Word that was sent for you.

Prayer: Send Your Word, O Lord

Father of Mercy,
You sent Your Word and healed them,
Not by formula, but by faith.
Not by proximity, but by promise.

Send Your Word to me today,
Into the places I cannot reach.
Into the wounds I cannot name.
Into the fears I cannot face.

Let Your Word be my medicine.
Let it deliver me from destruction,
From despair, from confusion, from every lie of the enemy.

Jesus, Living Word,
Speak healing into my body.
Speak peace into my mind.
Speak identity into my soul.

Holy Spirit,
Make the Word alive in me.
Let it dwell richly.
Let it restore deeply.
Let it deliver completely.

I receive Your Word,
Not just as text, but as truth.
Not just as doctrine, but as destiny.
Not just as comfort, but as a calling.
Amen.

> *Isaiah 43:1 KJV—* "*Fear not, for I have redeemed thee, I have called thee by thy name, thou art mine.*"

God does not speak in vague generalities. He calls you by name. You are not anonymous to God. He created you. He formed you. He redeemed you. And He calls you His. This is more than identity; it is intimacy. You are not a number, a diagnosis, or a statistic. You are His.

When the world labels you by your weakness, God names you by your worth. When destruction tries to define you, God's Word reclaims you. He does not simply know your name; He speaks it with love, with purpose, and with power. You belong to Him. That belonging is your healing and your identity.

Prayer: You Call Me Yours

Lord God,
You created me, not by accident, but by intention.
You formed me not only physically but also spiritually.
You redeemed me, not with silver or gold,
But with the precious blood of Your Son.

You call me by name,
Not the name the world gave me,
But the name You whispered before I was born.

I am Yours.
Not because I earned it,
But because You declared it.

Let Your Word silence every lie.
Let Your voice drown out every fear.
Let Your name be over me,
My healing, my identity, my legacy.

I receive Your Word today,
The Word that calls me beloved, chosen, redeemed.
Amen.

> *Romans 12:2 KJV— "Be ye transformed by the renewing of your mind…"*

This above verse is a cornerstone for understanding transformation through the Word. It is not about external behavior modification, but internal renewal. Transformation begins in the mind. The world tries to shape us through fear, comparison, and distraction. The Word of God renews us, restoring clarity, identity, and purpose.

To be transformed is to be re-formed by truth. The Word rewrites our thoughts, reframes our desires, and realigns our will with the will of God. This is not passive change. It is active surrender. The Word does not simply inform. It reforms. It not only teaches. It transforms. As your mind is renewed, your life begins to reflect the will of God, which is good, acceptable, and perfect.

The Word as Healing and Identity

The Word Heals What the World Cannot

The world may offer sympathy, but the Word offers restoration. Healing in Scripture is not only physical. It is emotional, spiritual, and relational. The Word enters wounds, not to observe them, but to mend them. Psalm 107:20 declares that God "sent his word, and healed them". The Word does not avoid brokenness. It seeks it. It speaks life into places others have abandoned. It does not simply treat symptoms. It transforms the soul. Healing is not always the removal of pain. It is often the revelation of purpose within it. The Word does not always erase wounds. It sanctifies them.

The Word Renames You

In Scripture, transformation often arrives with a new name.

- Abram becomes Abraham
- Jacob becomes Israel
- Simon becomes Peter
- Saul becomes Paul

These changes reveal identity shifts initiated by divine encounters. The Word of God speaks not only to who you are, but to whom you are becoming. Your past does not define you, your pain, or your paralysis. You are defined by the Word that calls you forward into a new identity and a new future.

The Word Renews the Mind

Transformation begins in the mind. The Word rewrites internal scripts of shame, fear, and defeat. It replaces lies with truth, confusion with clarity, and despair with hope. Romans 12:2 calls us to be transformed by the renewing of our minds. Healing is not only recovery. It is renewal. Identity is not only discovered. It is declared. The Word does both. It reveals who God is and, in doing so, reveals who you are in Him.

The Word Is Living and Active

The Word of God is not a relic. It is a force. Hebrews 4:12 tells us that the Word of God is quick and powerful, sharper than any two-edged sword. It cuts through confusion, exposes falsehood, and affirms truth. It is not passive. It is powerful.

- When you read the Word, it reads you
- When you speak the Word, it shapes you
- When you believe the Word, it heals you

The Word That Rewrites the Story

The Word of God is a narrative force. It reframes your testimony. What was once a story of suffering becomes a story of glory. Quadriplegia becomes a platform for Anastasia to rise again. The

Word does not merely interpret your life. It authors it. Isaiah 61:3 promises beauty for ashes, the oil of joy for mourning, and the garment of praise for the spirit of heaviness. The Word of God is the pen that rewrites your identity. You are not a victim. You are a vessel.

The Word That Dwells Within

Healing and identity are sustained by intimacy with the Word. The Spirit activates the Word within you. Scripture is not only external truth. It becomes an internal transformation.

> Galatians 2:20 declares, *"I am crucified with Christ. Nevertheless, I live. Yet not I, but Christ liveth in me."*

Transformation is not self-improvement. It is self-surrender. Paul testifies that his old self is crucified with Christ. What remains is not ego, but embodiment. Christ living within.

This is the mystery of identity in the Word. Your past no longer defines you, your pain, or your paralysis. You are defined by the One who lives in you. The life you now live is not powered by performance, but by faith in the Son of God, who loves you and gave Himself for you. This is not mere theology. It is testimony. You are not only alive. You are indwelt. Transformation is not behavior modification. It is spiritual rebirth. The Word lives in you, speaks through you, and shapes your legacy.

Prayer: Speak Healing, Speak Identity

Lord,
You are the Word that heals,
The Voice that restores,
The Name Giver who redefines.

You do not speak to impress. You speak to transform.
You do not whisper to inform. You whisper to awaken.

Speak into my broken places,
Not with condemnation, but with compassion.
Not with diagnosis, but with destiny.

Let Your Word be balm to my wounds,
Bread to my hunger,
Breath to my stillness.

Call me by the name You chose,
Not the name the world gave,
Not the name my suffering echoes,
But the name written in Your heart.

Let me hear You say,
Beloved. Healed. Whole. Mine.

Let Your Word rewrite my story.
Let Your Spirit renew my mind.
Let Your truth restore my identity.

I am not what I lost.
I am not what I cannot do.
I am who You say I am.

So, I rise,
Not in strength, but in surrender.
Not in pride, but in promise.
Not in fear, but in faith.

Speak again, Lord.
And I will be healed.
And I will be named.
And I will be Yours.
Amen.

Personal Notes

CHAPTER 12

Anastasia, The Word That Raises

Anastasia means resurrection. It is not just a theological concept. It is a lived reality. This chapter is not about standing by strength, but by the Spirit. It is not about recovery alone, but about revelation. From the stillness of quadriplegia to the stirring of divine identity, Anastasia is the moment the Word speaks again, not only to heal, but to raise. It is the call to rise, not merely from affliction, but into assignment.

In the biblical witness, resurrection is not simply life restored. It is life transformed and purpose redefined.

- Lazarus did not only walk out of the tomb, but he also became a testimony.
- Jairus' daughter not only woke up, but she became a witness.
- Jesus did not only rise, but He ascended, commissioned, and empowered.

Anastasia is rising. It is the moment when the Word of God calls you by name, breathes into your being, and says, "Stand up." Not because you are strong, but because He is. Not because you are ready, but because He is faithful. Not because you understand, but because you are chosen.

In seasons of suffering, the letter may feel heavy, but the Spirit gives breath. The Word is not only a doctrine to recite. It is a presence to receive. When the body fails, when the mind is weary, when the heart is broken, the Spirit animates the Word with resurrection power. You are not a minister of rules. You are a minister of life. Not of condemnation, but of compassion. Not of law, but of love. The same Spirit that raised Jesus from the dead dwells in you. He quickens your mortal body. He revives your soul. He speaks through your story.

This chapter is a declaration. You are not defined by what holds you down. You are defined by the Word that lifts you.

> *Ephesians 2:1-6 KJV* — *"And you hath he quickened… and hath raised us up together, and made us sit together in heavenly places in Christ Jesus."*

You were once dead, not only physically limited, but spiritually disconnected. You walked according to patterns that did not reflect heaven. But God, rich in mercy, did not leave you there. He quickened you. He revived you. He restored you. He resurrected you. This is Anastasia.

- Not only standing up, but being raised with Christ.
- Not only surviving, but reigning.
- Not only healing, but ascending.

Your past walk, your former pain, and your earthly limitations no longer define you. You are seated with Christ, positioned in heavenly places, clothed in grace, and empowered by love. This is your new identity. Alive. Raised. Enthroned.

Prayer: Raise Me, Seat Me, Use Me

Father of Mercy,
You saw me in my deadness,
In my sin, in my sorrow, in my silence.
And You quickened me.

You raised me with Christ.
You seated me in heavenly places.
I receive this resurrection life,
Not by merit, but by mercy.
Not by strength, but by grace.

Let me walk in this newness.
Let me live from this position.
Let me speak from this identity.

Jesus, You stood up from the grave.
Now raise me to stand in purpose.
Let Anastasia be more than recovery.
Let it be a resurrection into calling.
Amen.

> Galatians 4:7 KJV — "Thou art no more a servant, but a son... an heir of God through Christ."

This verse is a profound affirmation of identity and inheritance. It speaks directly to the heart of transformation. You are no longer bound by fear, performance, or spiritual slavery. You are welcomed into divine sonship. You are not merely tolerated. You are treasured. You are not only forgiven. You are adopted. Through Christ, you have been raised from the dust of servanthood to the dignity of sonship.

This is the essence of Anastasia

- Not only standing up, but stepping into your inheritance.
- You are an heir, not of earthly riches, but of divine promises.
- You are no longer striving for approval. You are living from acceptance.

The Word has spoken your identity. The Spirit confirms it. You are a child of God. You are His.

> *John 11:25 KJV — "I am the resurrection, and the life…"*

This verse is the heartbeat of Anastasia. Jesus not only offers resurrection. He is resurrection. He is the life that overcomes death. He is the Word that calls the dead to rise. He is the voice that awakens destiny. When He speaks, tombs tremble. When He calls, grave clothes fall. When He arrives, mourning turns into movement.

This is Anastasia

- Not only standing up, but being called out.
- Not only surviving, but living again, entirely, freely, and faithfully.

You may feel buried by circumstance, but Jesus is nearby. He is the resurrection and the life. Believe, and live. Anastasia is the declaration that your story did not end in the valley. It rises on the mountain. It speaks of grace, glory, and the God who lifts. You are not only walking again. You are walking in resurrection light.

Anastasia is not merely a theological truth. It is a personal testimony. To stand up is to step into a new story. Yet every resurrection invites reflection. What does it mean to rise? What does it mean to walk again, not only physically, but spiritually, emotionally, and relationally? The Word that raised you now walks with you. As you move forward, your experience becomes sacred ground. It is not only a moment of healing, but a journey of becoming. Not only a miracle witnessed, but a message lived.

In the next chapter, we pause to honor the individual experience, the unique way God speaks, heals, and reveals Himself in your life. This is where resurrection becomes relationship. Where standing up becomes walking with God. Look for the Word. It will find you.

Reflection Point

Anastasia calls the reader to see resurrection as a present reality, not just a past event. In Christ, life is no longer defined by affliction, limitation, or past patterns, but by being raised, seated, and loved as a son and heir of God. The same Spirit that raised Jesus now calls each believer by name—out of fear, shame, and stagnation—into movement, purpose, and intimate partnership with God. Resurrection, then, is more than healing; it is a new identity and a continual walk in resurrection light.

Prayer: Call Me Out, O Resurrection

Jesus,
You are the resurrection and the life.
You do not only restore. You revive.
You do not only comfort. You call.

Call me out of every grave,
Graves of fear, shame, silence, and sorrow.
Speak life into my spirit.
Speak movement into my stillness.
Speak purpose into my pain.

I believe in You,
Not only as Savior, but as Resurrection.
Raise me to walk again.
Raise me to live again.
Raise me to love again.

Let Anastasia be my testimony,
That I was dead, but now I live.
That I was silent, but now I speak.
That I was broken, but now I rise.

Let Your Word be the breath that lifts me,
From paralysis to praise.
Amen.

CHAPTER 13

Individual Experience
When the Word Speaks Your Name

"Richard Akintayo, in the name of JESUS of Nazareth, rise up and walk."

Deuteronomy 11:18 NIV — "Fix these words of mine in your hearts and minds…"

There are moments when the Word of God stops being general and becomes personal. Moments when it does not simply echo through Scripture, but speaks your name. This was one of those moments—a moment when heaven interrupted earth. A Word was spoken. A name was called. A life was redefined.

In the book of Acts, Peter spoke to the lame man at the temple gate and said, "In the name of Jesus Christ of Nazareth, rise up and walk." That same Word echoed into my story. Not as a metaphor, but as a miracle. Not as encouragement, but as empowerment.

This chapter honors my personal encounter, the moment when the Word became flesh in my life, when paralysis met prophecy, when silence met Spirit, when the name of JESUS rewrote my identity. Individual experience is where theology becomes testimony. It is where the Word of God speaks not only to the world, but to me. It is where resurrection becomes relationship, where healing becomes heritage. Where standing up becomes stepping forward.

This is my story: Not only of what happened, but of what was spoken. Not only of what I endured, but of what I became. I rose, not by strength, but by the name above all names, the name of JESUS CHRIST.

In the Beginning, A Legacy of the Word

I was born on September 28, 1954, in Lagos, Nigeria, which served as the nation's capital from 1914 to 1991. My earliest introduction to the Word of God came through my beloved mother, Madam Hannah Yetunde Ejide Alli Balogun. She was the eldest daughter of Busari Alli Balogun, the second Balogun of Lagos, who succeeded his father, Sheikh Makanjuola Alli Balogun (fondly known as Alli Oloko), the first Balogun of Lagos.

My mother was born into Islam but later embraced Christianity. She worshipped at The Apostolic Church Nigeria, whose Lagos headquarters stood at 45 Cemetery Street. I was the youngest of her four children, a child of "old age." My father was 48, and my mother was 42 when I was born, with a 20-year gap between my eldest sibling.

Her zeal for the LORD was unmatched. Our home became a sanctuary of prayer, a place where people came to seek divine counsel and draw from her spiritual gifts. She was generous and hospitable, often hosting guests beyond our immediate family. At The Apostolic Church, it was customary for congregants to gather at the national headquarters in Lagos to fast and pray as they awaited the Word of the Year. This divine motto would guide their faith and endeavors. My mother ensured that every member of our household participated, and we would not break our fast until the Word was received. This spiritual discipline laid the foundation for my own pursuit of GOD.

> *Proverbs 22:6. KJV — "Train up a child in the way he should go, and when he is old, he will not depart from it."*

Beyond prayer, my mother loved to worship through song. She had favorite hymns she chanted daily and insisted that I say a short prayer before school, often accompanied by canticles. This nurtured in me a habit of murmuring worship songs throughout the day.

My Daily Anthem

During my high school years, one song became my daily anthem:

> *"Father, lead me day by day,*
> *Ever in Thine own sweet way.*
> *Teach me to be pure and true,*
> *Show me what I ought to do..."*

I especially cherished the second stanza:

"When in danger, make me brave,
Make me know that Thou canst save.
Keep me safe by Thy dear side,
Let me in Thy love abide."
— *"A Child's Prayer for Guidance"* by John Hopps.

My mother also counselled me with the wisdom of King Lemuel's mother, as found in Proverbs 31:1-9. I vividly recall one walk home from church when she asked me to promise to remain in the Christian faith and to read the Bible diligently. She told me this was the path to prosperity and good success, a truth I later discovered in Joshua 1:8.

That day, she also spoke prophetic words over my siblings, entrusting me with messages for each of them. I did not realize then that she was giving me her parting words. She passed away a few months later, on March 5, 1968, at the age of 56. I was just 13 years old and in high school. She had been battling cancer for two years. Her bedside nurse told us that in her final moments, she cried out in agony and asked the LORD to open the gates of paradise, and her request was granted.

Heaven gained her sweet soul. We lost a spiritual matriarch. But what she sowed in me bore fruit. Her prophetic words about my brother came to pass, and he confirmed them before his passing in 2003. Throughout my school years, I continued the spiritual routines she had instilled in me, especially during examinations.

Charles Wesley's hymn became my exam day declaration:

"Forth in Thy name, O Lord, I go,
My daily labor to pursue.
Thee, only Thee, resolved to know,
In all I think or speak or do."
—Charles Wesley

I later learned that this hymn reflects a Christian's dedication to serving GOD in every aspect of daily life. My mother taught me to seek the Word through prayer and fasting. She spoke life over her children in alignment with Scripture, and those words did not return void (Isaiah 55:11). She also spoke life into me, and I am the living fruit of the power of her tongue, enabled by the Holy Spirit. Her words were sweet and pure. She harbored no bitterness.

Job 42:5 KJV — "I had heard of You by the hearing of the ear…".

Indeed, the Word was introduced to me through my mother's teachings, her lifestyle, and the songs and hymns that filled our home, habitually.

Life Journey, From Drifting to Destiny

After my mother passed away, I drifted into what I now call "playing religion." I mouthed scriptures without truly committing to the Word. I left The Apostolic Church, first joining the Methodist Church, then the Anglican Communion, likely influenced by our mission schoolteachers. The pull of the world was strong, and distractions abounded. Church attendance became a chore.

Devotion gradually faded. The vortex was real. But for the mercies of GOD, I would have been consumed.

Later, I found this truth beautifully expressed in Lamentations 3:22: "It is of the LORD's mercies that we are not consumed, because His compassions fail not." GOD's love is steadfast. He loved us first and continues to love His creation. He waits with open arms to receive us.

This truth became evident in 1980 during my postgraduate studies at the University of Bradford in West Yorkshire, England. Some Jamaican college mates invited me into a campus Christian fellowship affiliated with the Baptist Church. We gathered for house fellowship on Thursdays and attended church on Sundays. It was a season of soul searching that culminated in my baptism in April 1981. That baptism came with a certificate and a life-defining scripture:

> *Galatians 4:7 NIV* — *"So, you are no longer a slave, but God's child, and since you are His child, God has made you also an heir."*

The year 1981 was pivotal. I graduated from university and also met Maureen Olayinka Akinbola, who would become my wife and the mother of our four children. I had felt a nudge to visit my friend, Engr. Bayo Adebowale, who was pursuing his PhD at Imperial College London. I left Bradford and headed to Bayo's residence, unaware that he had just met Maureen at Shepherd's Bush Market and was returning with her.

Maureen is the elder sister of Titi, who was Toks' classmate, Toks being Bayo's girlfriend and later his wife. That divine appointment led to our union in 1984.

> *Romans 11:33 to 36 NIV—* "*Oh, the depth of the riches of the wisdom and knowledge of God. How unsearchable His judgments, and His paths beyond tracing out.*"

My obedience to that inner prompting brought Maureen and me together in holy matrimony. Maureen's parents were Catholics, so before our wedding, we underwent marriage preparation at Holy Cross Cathedral in Lagos. These premarital classes included inventories and counselling sessions and emphasized that marriage is a lifelong sacrament, a sacred covenant between man and woman. It is a partnership oriented toward mutual good and the nurturing of children. The union reflects Christ's love for the Church and calls for exclusive fidelity and openness to life. That preparation drew us deeper into the Word.

One cherished moment from our wedding was the repeated admonition from my elder cousin, Mr. Bode Akintayo, who was 22 years my senior. Throughout the evening, he would say, "Richard, marriage is patience." Those words etched themselves into my soul. They became a guiding principle in our marriage and a message I have passed on to our children and to those I have counselled. His words were not just advice. They were a blessing.

The Power of Names and Monikers

Another profound lesson I have learned in life is the power of names. I recall the story of Jacob's last son, whom Rachel named

Benoni, "Son of my sorrow", but Jacob renamed him Benjamin, "Son of my right hand", a shift from sorrow to strength. Similarly, Jabez, whose name meant "he causes pain", cried out to the GOD of Israel for blessing, expansion, divine presence, and protection. Scripture records that GOD granted his request and that he became more honorable than his brothers.

I have seen how college nicknames such as "Enjoyment", "Jesus' Child", "Devil Child", "Snake", and "Aristo" played out in the lives of those who bore them. Words carry weight. Names shape destiny. In many cultures, naming is sacred. Scripture teaches that names reveal character, calling, and spiritual identity.

> *Proverbs 18:10 — "The name of the LORD is a strong tower; the righteous run to it and are safe."*

We took great care in naming our children, speaking inspired words over them from birth:

Samuel, "God hears."
A dependable, wise, and responsible leader. Our Samuel was commissioned to feed our sheep and tend our lambs, his siblings.

Emmanuel, "God with us."
Confident, courageous, and justice-driven. We often declared, "Emmanuel, God is with you," as he stepped into new frontiers.

Gabriel, "God's Personal Messenger."
Purposeful, kind, and obedient to divine instruction. We affirmed, "Gabriel, you are a carrier of good news."

Hannah, "Grace or Favor of God."
Resilient, prayerful, and faithful. We would say, "Hannah prays, and God answers."

These names were not mere labels. They were declarations. Our children grew up carrying the weight and wonder of those words.

The Word in the Name
GOD is faithful, loving, merciful, and strong. His name is a refuge and a fortress.

Emmanuel, "God is with us."

El Roi, "The GOD who sees."

Look to see the One who sees you. The Word is revealed in the person of JESUS CHRIST, called The Word. So, look and see JESUS CHRIST.

The Catastrophic Incident, The Valley and the Voice

I have been privileged to sit at the feet of Rev. Chris Okotie, Shepherd Superintendent of the Household of GOD Church in Lagos, and to drink from the wellspring of wisdom poured out by Pastor Tunde Bakare, founding overseer of Citadel Global Community Church. In the United States, I worshipped at Victory Church in Norcross and drew profound inspiration from Pastor Michael Todd of Transformation Church in Tulsa. The spiritual enlightenment I received from these encounters became an anchor for my soul during what I now call "The Catastrophic Incident."

It began in May 2023, in Lagos, Nigeria. An excruciating pain in my neck suddenly gripped me. Concerned, I went to the hospital, where an MRI scan of my spine was ordered. As I lay inside the machine, the rhythmic pounding echoed in my ears, eerily reminiscent of the dirge *"Papa is being taken home."* In that moment, it felt as though the enemy whispered, *"You are going to die."* But I knew it was a lie from the pit of hell.

Two days into my hospital stay, I heard a voice, clear and unmistakable: **"Richard Akintayo, in the name of JESUS of Nazareth, rise up and walk."** It was perplexing, even surreal, because I was still walking. Yet I knew this was not a statement about my present. It was a divine declaration for the days ahead. I treasured that Word in my heart.

The Journey Begins

After four days, I was discharged to continue treatment in the United States. On the way to the airport, Dr. Gboyega Oke, my wife, and I stopped briefly at home. A brother from my Lagos church came by to assist with personal needs. As we drove out of the estate, we passed him again. I heard the words, "Did you see your brother?" I responded inwardly, "He looked worn out and dejected." And instantly, I knew what I was being prompted to do.

We arrived in Atlanta, Georgia, on June 8, 2023, and I went straight to the hospital. Just two days later, I experienced a sudden and complete paralysis of all four limbs, quadriplegia. Only my voice remained. But GOD had preserved my mouth as a weapon of praise. So, I sang a song from the Household of GOD Church.

"With my lips, I will bless Thee,
With my mouth, I sing Your praise.
With my eyes, I long to see You, show me Your face.
With my ears, I want to hear You.
With my hands, I want to touch You.
With my heart, I surrender all to You."

In that place of stillness and surrender, I remembered the Word I had received in Lagos: "Richard Akintayo, in the name of JESUS of Nazareth, rise up and walk."

> *Isaiah 43:1 KJV— "Fear not, for I have redeemed thee, I have called thee by thy name, thou art mine."*

That Word became my anthem, my meditation, my lifeline. I clung to it with unwavering faith.

> *Deuteronomy 11:18 NIV— "Fix these words of mine in your hearts and minds."*

Surgery, Suffering, and Songs

I was transferred to **Emory University Hospital in Midtown Atlanta,** where my first surgery took place early Sunday morning, **June 11, 2023.** According to the medical report, I awoke saying, "Thank You, JESUS."

> *1 Thessalonians 5:18 KJV— "In everything give thanks."*

Later, I read the Spiritual Health Note and realized my wife had been teary. What she needed most in that moment was not words, but presence, someone to be with her. She found relief when the LORD was invoked into her space.

> *Psalm 34:18 NIV— "The LORD is close to the brokenhearted and saves those who are crushed in spirit."*

After surgery, I was moved to the ICU. When I opened my eyes, I saw my children. Their presence gave me strength and encouragement. They were indeed arrows in my hands.

> *Psalm 127:3 - 5 KJV — "Lo, children are a heritage of the LORD… Happy is the man that hath his quiver full of them."*

They left their lives behind and stayed with me for weeks. I remembered Sister Teena, who had grounded them in the Word at the Children's Church of the Household of GOD Church. May GOD bless her for the foundation she laid. They honored us, their parents, and we prayed that it would be well with them, that their days would be long.

> *Ephesians 6:2 to 3 KJV— "Honor thy father and mother… that it may be well with thee."* .

On **June 16, Rev. Chris Okotie's birthday,** I underwent a second surgery. I sensed a divine assurance. It was a gift of healing on his birthday. My wife prayed fervently, using me as a point of contact for others in the ICU. Testimonies abounded. **El Roi** saw her and dispensed grace.

Later, I was moved to **Room 308.** I saw "3" as divine perfection and "8" as new beginnings. I believed I would witness a perfect new beginning in health. One day, I released my faith by chanting **"JESUS" seventy times** while trying to move my right leg. At the seventieth shout, sensation returned.

> *Psalm 50:15 KJV— "Call upon Me in the day of trouble…"*

The name JESUS was the mystery in the miracle. I glorified GOD the Almighty.

As physical and occupational therapists began working on my limbs, I became intensely aware of the magnitude of GOD's deliverance from death.

Job 33:24 KJV — "Then He is gracious unto him, and saith, deliver him from going down to the pit, I have found a ransom."

Thank You, JESUS. You are the ransom.

Faith, Family, and Fruitfulness

Visitors began to arrive. **Dr. Fred and Tutu Tega, Shola and Fisayo Omojokun, Grandma Sanusi, Mrs. Tutu Ayeni, Dr. Biodun Kuku, Demi, "my Prof" Anjola, and my praise partner Tobi,** each one a vessel of grace. After my discharge, Shola and Fisayo took us to **Victory Church in Norcross** every Sunday. The seeds sown in childhood had borne fruit.

At a stage in **Room 308**, I looked at my daughter and said, "I will walk you down the aisle." It was not a fantasy. It was faith speaking. A seed sown in love, watered by belief. Later, I sent her "I'm Blessed" by Charlie Wilson, the song I envision us dancing to on her wedding day.

The Shepherd and the Stretch

After five weeks, I was admitted to the **Shepherd Centre** for spinal cord rehabilitation. My wife and children ensured I received the best care. They were my advocates, my intercessors, my family. I was received into **Room 506, "5"** for grace and **"6"** for man. I, a man, had found grace.

The name **"Shepherd Centre"** spoke to me. I remembered:

- The **Good Shepherd**
- The **Great Shepherd**
- The **Chief Shepherd**

I sang:

"Shepherd of my soul, I give You full control…"

I knew I was in the valley and that the LORD JESUS was by my side. Grace was dispensed to me, and the LORD JESUS became my ransom.

> *Job 33:24 KJV—"Deliver him from going down to the pit, I have found a ransom."*

Pain and Praise

A high-level evaluation was conducted. The treatment plan was shared. I believed in a positive result. Yet the six weeks were filled with challenges. I was confined to a wheelchair. Pain surged to ten out of ten during transfers. I began to say, "LORD JESUS, take my pain as I do the roller coaster." That became my way of managing the pain, entrusting it to the Shepherd of my soul.

I looked at myself, bony, frail, unable to hold silverware. I was despondent. Then came a voice. **Dr. Tega** said, **"Uncle Rich, I have never seen you like this."** His words were not condemnation. They were a mirror. And in that mirror, I saw not only my condition, but my covenant.

Psalm 30:5 — "Weeping may endure for a night, but joy cometh in the morning."

Like a deer panting for water, my soul began to pant for the LORD. I hummed the melody of **Psalm 42** and cried out from the depths. I found peace.

That very evening, the LORD sent tokens of His love. "My Prof", Anjola, brought me apple pie, my favorite dessert. Grandma Sanusi and Mrs. Tutu Ayeni came bearing warm, home-cooked meals. My palate opened. My appetite returned. My body responded. Healing had begun.

The Stirring

In the quiet of recovery, I remembered a stirring from Lagos, my brother in the church. Before I left Nigeria, the LORD had placed him on my heart. I said to the LORD, "I want to support him, but I need my hands to make the transfers." That very day, my hands were restored. I made the first transfer. It was not just a transaction. It was a testimony. Hallelujah.

Room 506 became a sanctuary. Through the long nights, my wife, Maureen, would strengthen herself by playing "Lead Me Lord" by Gary Valenciano. The first stanza ministered deeply and became our shared prayer:

> *"Lead me, Lord,*
> *Lead me by the hand and help me face the rising sun.*
> *Comfort me through all the pain that life may bring.*
> *There's no other hope that I can lean on.*
> *Lead me, Lord, lead me all my life."*

I offered praise songs to the LORD, inviting His Spirit into our space, enthroning JESUS as King and LORD over everything. Among many songs, I sang:

- *"Emmanuel, My GOD Is Here."*
- *"Shiloh, You Are My Tranquillizer."*
- *"Hail JESUS Is LORD."*
- *"JESUS Is Praying, I Know HE Is Praying for You."*
- *"LORD, You Are So Beautiful."*
- *"He'll Send the WORD and Make You Whole."*
- *"JESUS, We Enthrone You, We Proclaim You Are King."*

These songs became my medicine, words of strength, hope, peace, comfort, deliverance, and healing. Each song was a sword: each lyric, a ladder.

I graduated from the Shepherd Centre's Inpatient program and moved into a nearby senior living apartment for Day and Outpatient therapy. I honor my wife for her obedience to the instructions I gave during my hospitalization, even though it later came at a cost. She is a divine gift to me, sent by GOD for such a time as this.

I also remember my sister-in-law, **Mrs. Mary Coker,** whose counsel in Brighton, England, still echoes in my heart: **"Now that you are married, do not allow anything or anyone to come between you and her."** I defended my wife for carrying out those instructions, and with GOD as our anchor, we became a threefold cord that could not be broken. Together, we waded through the storm of my affliction, upheld by grace and bound by covenant.

Ecclesiastes 4:12 NIV — *"Though one may be overpowered, two can defend themselves. A cord of three strands is not quickly broken."*

Rev. Chris Okotie prayed for me often and taught me the principle of "Ten Toes." During therapy, I stood on terra firma and by faith declared, "I will rise up and walk." I held on to that Word. On August 6, 2023, **Pastor Tunde Bakare** prayed for me during his church service, echoing Peter's words to Aeneas in Acts 9:34, to decree my healing. He later visited me in Atlanta with his wife.

Mr. Lekan Adebiyi also visited around that time to strengthen me. Many speculated about the cause of my affliction, curses, enchantments, divinations, but I was unmoved. I had heard a WORD in Lagos that became my faith confession: "Richard Akintayo, in the name of JESUS of Nazareth, rise and walk."

Later, I listened to **Pastor Michael Todd's "Faith Talk"** sermon from Transformation Church in Tulsa. It confirmed what I already knew.

I anchored myself in the mercy of GOD, singing:

> *"HIS death gives us a second chance,*
> *HIS life gives us a place with GOD,*
> *HIS word gives us promises and hope,*
> *HIS compassion will never fail.*
> *Loving kindness HE gives to us all.*
> *HE knows we are just children, so weak.*
> *He'll never leave you, He'll never leave me.*
> *He'll always be there."*

Chorus:
"What a GOD of mercy HE is,
What a GOD of mercy HE is.
HE forgives iniquity, forgives transgressions,
Reserves mercy for thousands.

Help me, O LORD, to be the one whose mind is always stayed upon YOU,
To bring glory and honor to YOUR name.
YOUR mercy, LORD, has touched my heart.
There is nothing I will not do to show how much I love YOU.
He'll never leave you; He'll never leave me.
He'll always be there."
— Household of GOD

I completed my rehabilitation at Shepherd Centre on December 21, 2023.

Year 2024, From Ashes to Ascension

There are seasons when the soul walks through fire, when grief clings like ash and injustice presses like iron. The year began in shadows. Bereavement tore through hearts. Persecution silenced voices. Oppression weighed heavily on the spirit. It felt as though hope had been buried beneath the rubble of despair.

But thorns, though cruel, are not the end of the story. In the furnace of affliction, faith is tempered. In the silence of sorrow, heaven whispers resurrection.

I knew a man who glimpsed the third heaven, and unlike Paul, he longed to stay and begin eternity. That man was my brother-in-law, **Anthony Akinniyi Akinbola.** Even on his hospital bed, he preached the fidelity of GOD and the hope of eternal life. We lost him on Friday, January 26, 2024, and the entire family was plunged into mourning. Our spirits were low. Our hearts were grieving as a family.

As if that loss was not enough, waves of oppression and persecution followed. In my state of health and bereavement, I expected empathy, but instead, I was afflicted. Their heels were raised against me. Grief carved deep hollows in my heart, and persecution whispered lies that I was forgotten. Oppression pressed not only from the outside, but from within. I questioned my strength, my faith, and my purpose.

Each step was heavy with sorrow. Each breath became a prayer for relief. I wept in my wheelchair and asked, "Why me? Why all this at this age?" My tears watered the dust beneath me, and I wondered if anything good could grow in such a barren place.

Psalm 120:7 — "I am for peace, but when I speak, they are for war."

So, I gave myself to prayer. GOD does not waste tears. They are liquid prayers. Somewhere in the silence, hope began to stir, not loudly, not all at once, but like a hidden spring breaking through cracked earth. The valley did not change overnight, but I did. I began to see beauty in broken places. Strength rose from the soil of suffering. The weeping did not vanish. It was transformed.

What once felt like exile became an encounter. Spring flowed not despite the tears, but because of them.

I remembered Job's endurance, Jacob's wrestling, and Joseph's journey, all of which ended in praise. I prayed for mercy for us all. I smiled as I recalled my late brother, **Donald Babatunde Coker**, my mentor and primary caregiver after our mother's passing. His words still echo: *"Richard, don't worry yourself. Time has a way of healing all wounds. It has a way of sorting things out."* I thank GOD for the beautiful moments we shared.

There were remnants GOD had prepared for such a time. My brother's daughters, **Anne and Peju**, would call often, stirring the spirit of camaraderie. **Biola Balogun** would do likewise. My in-law, **Tayo Ayeni**, flew in from Nigeria multiple times. **Bola Odusi** and **Ikepo Osawaiye** visited twice from Canada. **Dr. Biodun Kuku** visited us three times from Monroe, Louisiana, and shared his knowledge. **Mike Igbokwe SAN** ministered the Scriptures faithfully with grace.

Jerry Onifade introduced me to **"Fully Restored" and "8 Hours of Healing Scriptures" by Pastor Joseph Prince.** Updates from Household of GOD Church came through Ronke Adewale, Head of Benevolence. **Victory Church Norcross** was a blessing. **Hajia Maryam Uwais** visited from Nigeria. My in-laws were always present.

Ayo Lawson would drive an hour to pick up my wife and me, cook Nigerian meals, and return us to our senior living apartment. GOD has recorded his labor of love. **Bayo Adebowale** checked in consistently. The LORD will be there for him.

I must also honor **Pastor Tunde, Mrs. Laiye Bakare, Mr. Lekan**, and **Mrs. Lara Adebiyi,** who flew in multiple times from Nigeria and witnessed my healing journey. I pray over the houses of Bakare and Adebiyi, blessing them with the blessing of **2 Timothy 1:16-18**. I also acknowledge **Rev. Chris Okotie's** fidelity.

Throughout this season, GOD stood solidly with us. He gave me the words, the inspiration, the style, the pattern, and the blueprint for every situation.

> *Job 33:15 to 16 KJV* — *"In a dream, in a vision of the night, when deep sleep falleth upon men, in slumbering upon the bed, Then He openeth the ears of men, and sealeth their instruction."*

I would sleep, and GOD would reveal what to do. I would then locate the appropriate Scripture to confirm it. Precept upon precept, line upon line, here a little and there a little, the Word of the LORD was upon me.

Later that year, stirred by faith, I rose and cast aside my wheelchair, embracing the rolling walker and cane as living symbols of GOD's glory.

Today, I look back and see that the valley was not punishment. It was preparation. It was where my roots grew deep, where my faith was refined, where my joy was reborn. The valley of weeping became a spring. I am not the same. I underwent **four epidural procedures** and **two additional surgeries**.

This is my story. This is my testimony. That no darkness can extinguish the light of redemption. That no grave can hold what GOD has destined to rise, now, I rise, not only in body, but in testimony. I rise to declare that healing is possible, that faith still moves mountains, and that the Word of GOD is alive. My wheelchair was not the end. It was the altar. And from that altar, I stepped forward with a walker, a cane, and a calling.

To all who read this, your catastrophe is not your conclusion.
Look for the Word. Stand on it. Speak it. And when you do, you too will rise.

> Romans 8:11— "The Spirit of God, who raised Jesus from the dead, lives in you."

Prayer: You Spoke My Name

Jesus of Nazareth,
You did not only speak to the crowd, You spoke to me.
You not only healed the world, but You healed my story.

You called me by name,
And in Your name, I stood.

I thank You for the Word that found me,
For the voice that pierced my silence,
For the Spirit that raised me from stillness.

Let me never forget that moment,
When heaven spoke into my body,
When mercy rewrote my movement,
When grace gave me ground to walk on.

I walk now not in my own strength,
But in Your name.
I rise not by effort,
But by Your authority.

Let my life echo that Word.
Let my steps testify to Your power.
Let my story glorify Your name.

Amen.

CHAPTER 14

Conclusion
Look for the Word & Live the Word

This journey began with a whisper in the wilderness, a Word waiting to be found. It moved through creation, incarnation, healing, and resurrection, and now it arrives at a holy but straightforward call: to live. To look for the Word is to seek divine meaning. To live the Word is to embody divine purpose. It is not the end of the story but the beginning of a life shaped by revelation.

You have seen the Word in silence, in suffering, and in the Spirit. You have watched it call my name, raise my body, and renew my mind. Now, the invitation is clear. Let the Word become your walk. Let the Word become your witness. Let the Word become your way.

This chapter is a commissioning. It is not just a reminder of what God has spoken and done, but a call to respond with your life. To speak what He says. To move where He leads. To live as one transformed by truth. You are not only a reader of the Word; you are a carrier of it. You are not only a hearer; you are a living echo. Go forward. Look for the Word in every moment, and live it with every breath.

> *Revelation 19:13 KJV — "And he was clothed with a vesture dipped in blood: and his name is called The Word of God."*

This verse unveils the majesty of Christ in His triumphant return, clothed in sacrifice, crowned in authority, and named The Word of God. It is a powerful culmination of all we have been tracing. The Word is not only spoken; it is embodied. It is not only written; it is alive.

This Scripture is the final revelation of the One we have been seeking all along: not just a spoken Word, but a living, victorious King. He is clothed in sacrifice, crowned in glory, and named as The Word of God. To look for the Word is to seek Christ. To live the Word is to follow Him, not only in devotion, but in demonstration; not only in belief, but in becoming.

This verse reminds us that the Word is never passive. It is powerful. It walks into battle. It wears redemption. It carries authority. And now, as we conclude, we recognize that the Word we searched for is the One who saved us. The Word we lived by is the One who leads us. The Word we carry is the One who is coming again.

Let your life reflect His vesture. Let your walk echo His name. Let your legacy quietly declare, "I looked for the Word. I lived the Word. I followed the Word of God."

> *2 Corinthians 3:2–3 KJV — "Ye are our epistle written in our hearts... not with ink, but with the Spirit of the living God..."*

This passage beautifully affirms the heart of this conclusion. The

Word is not only written on pages; it is written on people. I am a living epistle. My quadriplegic journey, my resurrection testimony, my obedience to document this experience for others, all of it is the Spirit's ink on the tablet of my heart.

Here is the truth it confirms: legacy is not only taught; it is lived. The Word is not only spoken; it is embodied. You are not only a reader; you are a letter. Your life becomes a message that others can "read," one that points beyond you to the faithfulness of God.

> *John 6:68 KJV — "Lord, to whom shall we go? thou hast the words of eternal life."*

This verse reminds us that the Word is not just a source of comfort; it is the source of life itself. Peter's response is not cold theology. It is a cry from the heart of a man who has discovered that there is no other voice worth following.

The Word is not optional; it is essential. It is not only truth; it is life. To live the Word is to remain with the One who speaks eternal things, even when others turn away. All other paths eventually empty out. Only Christ's words lead to life that does not end.

> *Romans 12:1–2 KJV: — "I beseech you therefore, brethren, by the mercies of God, That ye present your bodies a living sacrifice, holy, acceptable unto God, which is your reasonable service. And be not conformed to this world: but be ye transformed by the renewing of your mind…"*

This passage is a powerful call to live the Word, not only in belief, but in embodiment. To live the Word is to place your body on the altar, even in weakness, as a living sacrifice. To live the Word is to resist the pressure of the world's patterns, and to embrace the slow, deep work of heaven's renewal.

My journey is a living witness to this transformation: from paralysis to purpose, from silence to surrender, from limitation to legacy. It is not only survival; it is service. It is not only recovery; it is revelation. The mercies of God became the reason and the strength to offer my life back to Him. The renewing of my mind, through the Word and the Spirit, became the proof that His will is good, acceptable, and perfect.

Look for the Word & Live the Word

To walk in the Word is to walk in the Spirit. The Spirit does not contradict the Word; He confirms it, empowers it, and applies it. When we read Scripture, we must invite the Spirit to breathe on it. When we speak Scripture, we must trust the Spirit to enforce it. When we live Scripture, we must rely on the Spirit to sustain it.

To look for the Word is to seek Christ. To live the Word is to become His witness. To look for the Word is to expect its confirmation, not always in thunder, but often in quiet transformation, not always in the dramatic, but in the daily. The Spirit still moves. The Word still speaks. God still bears witness.

To look for the Word is not merely to study doctrine, but to encounter the Divine. The Spirit breathes life into the Word, turning law into love, command into communion, and text into testimony. To look for the Word is to welcome both its fire and its hammer, to be refined, not just reassured, to be broken open so that healing can begin.

To look for the Word is to be armed with it. When you speak the Word, you strike with it. When you believe the Word, you are shielded by it. To look for the Word is to prepare the soil of your heart, to receive it with humility, to water it with prayer, to guard it with perseverance.

The Word heals by naming. It calls you beloved. It calls you chosen. It calls you whole. Your story may carry quadriplegia, wilderness seasons, or ashes of loss, but the Word speaks resurrection, identity, and purpose over you. Look for the Word. It will find you.

Prayer: Let Me Live the Word

Lord God,
You have spoken, and I have heard.
You have healed, and I have stood.
You have called, and I have answered.

Now let me live the Word,
Not just in devotion, but in decision.
Not just in prayer, but in practice.
Not just in silence, but in service.

Holy Spirit,
Write the Word on my heart.
Let it guide my steps,
Guard my speech,
And govern my soul.

*Let me be a living letter,
Known and read by all,
Pointing always to You.*

*Jesus, Word made flesh,
Let my life reflect Your truth,
Radiate Your grace,
And reveal Your glory.*

*I will look for the Word in every moment,
And I will live it with every breath.
Amen.*

Epilogue

Poetry of the Paralyzed

Legacy: A Generational Trust

From the beginning, God's covenant with Israel was never meant to be a private treasure; it was a generational trust. The Word was not just to be received. It was to be remembered, rehearsed, and relayed.

1. Deuteronomy 6:7—"Teach them diligently unto thy children…"
2. Exodus 20:6 — "Showing love to a thousand generations…"
3. Psalm 78:6— "Even children not yet born will rise and declare His praise."

This is the sacred rhythm of legacy:
- Receive the Word
- Live the Word
- Teach the Word

So that your children's children will not only know the stories of God, but will walk in them.

When my children asked me to document my quadriplegic experience for our grandchildren and others, I heard more than a request. I heard a divine instruction. It echoed the voice of God to the Israelites: *"Teach them diligently unto thy children… when thou sittest… walkest… liest down… risest up."*

Legacy is not just what we leave behind; it is what we pass forward. God instructed His people to remember, rehearse, and relay His wonders, to bind His Word on their hands, display it on their doorposts, and speak it in their homes.

Why?
- Because the Word must walk through generations.
- Because suffering must be redeemed through storytelling.
- Because healing must be handed down as heritage.

> *Psalm 145:4-7 KJV— "One generation shall praise thy works to another… They shall abundantly utter the memory of thy great goodness…"*

This is my offering to my children's children, to readers, and to generations of those who love the Lord:

- A record of grace amid limitation
- A witness of resurrection in the shadow of stillness
- A song from the soul when the body could not sing

I gave my heart to seek and search out, by the wisdom of God, the title for this book. I did not choose it lightly. I waited. I listened. I prayed. In the stillness, a phrase rose in my spirit, clear, weighty, and alive:

"Look for the Word."
- It was not just a title
- It was an instruction

- It was a revelation.
- It was the heartbeat of the journey I had lived through paralysis, silence, and resurrection.

"Look for the Word" became the lens through which I saw my suffering, my healing, and my calling.

It reminded me that even in the darkest places, the Word of God is present:
- Waiting to be found
- Waiting to be spoken to
- Waiting to rise

It also reminded me of my mum and the Apostolic Church days, when, through prayer and fasting, we sought the yearly WORD. It became the anchor for this book, the thread that ties every chapter, every prayer, every reflection, and my catastrophic experience.

This title is not just for me. It is for every reader, every seeker, every soul who has ever wondered if God still speaks. He does.

And if you look for the Word, you will find it:
- Not just in Scripture, but in silence
- Not just in healing, but in hardship
- Not just in movement, but in stillness

When you look for the Word, you realize **He has already been seeking you.** God is faithful. He loves you. In Him, you can become a new creation.

- **This book is my testimony**
- **This title is my obedience**
- **This Word is my witness**

Paralysis is often seen as silence — a place where movement ends and expression fades.

- But in the Spirit, even stillness speaks
- Even silence sings
- Even suffering writes

This epilogue is not a lament; it is a liturgy.

It is the poetry that rises from the places we thought were forgotten. It is the voice that emerges when the body cannot move, but the soul still leans in to hear the whisper of God.

The poetry of the paralyzed is not written with hands—
It is written with surrender.
It is not shaped by rhythm ;
It is shaped by revelation.
It is not bound by form ;
It is freed by faith.

- Here, the Word becomes whisper
- Here, the pain becomes praise
- Here, the stillness becomes a sanctuary

This is the final offering —
Not of strength, but of Spirit.
Not of resolution, but of resurrection.
Not of closure, but of communion.

Let these final words be a song from the soul, a testimony that even in paralysis, **the Word of God moves.**

Prayer: Word of Life, Walk With Me

Lord Jesus,
You are the Word I searched for,
The Word that found me,
The Word that healed me,
The Word that raised me.

From silence to speech,
From stillness to standing,
From brokenness to becoming,
You have walked with me through every page.

Now I ask:
Let me live the Word I have received.
Let it shape my thoughts,
Guide my steps,
And overflow in my witness.

Holy Spirit,
Let this devotional not be an ending,
But a beginning.
Let every reflection become revelation,
Every prayer becomes practice,
Every scripture becomes strength.

I commit my life to the Word,
To look for it in every moment,
To live it in every breath,
To share it with every soul You send.

Let my story echo Your truth.
Let my walk reflect Your glory.
Let my life be a living letter,
Written by Grace,
Read by others,
Rooted in You.

Amen.

Poetry of the Paralyzed

I do not walk, but I wander,
In the corridors of grace,
Where silence is a sermon
And breath becomes a hymn.

My limbs do not lift,
But my soul ascends,
On scaffolds of mercy
And ladders of light.

Pain is not the prison,
It is the prayer,
And the place where God
Whispers louder than thunder.

I have touched resurrection,
Not with fingers,
But with faith, it held me.

Stillness is a sanctuary.
Here, I rise.
Here, I walk.

Final Benediction

May the Word that spoke light into darkness, life into dust, and healing into affliction now speak into every reader's heart with resurrection power. May the same Spirit who raised Christ from the dead quicken your mortal body, renew your mind, and awaken your spirit to divine purpose. May you walk in the authority of the risen Christ, clothed in grace, anchored in truth, and ablaze with holy fire.

Finally, let every testimony in these pages become a seed for miracles, every reflection a doorway to intimacy with the Lord, and His Word, and every activation a call to destiny.

Go forth, healed, whole, and commissioned. In Jesus' name. Amen.

Numbers 6:24-26 KJV — "The Lord bless thee, and keep thee: The Lord make his face shine upon thee, and be gracious unto thee: The Lord lift up his countenance upon thee and give thee peace."

Personal Notes

NOTES & REFERENCE INDEX

Bible Versions

- KJV
- NIV
- CEV

Devotional Tools

- YouVersion (Daily Refresh and Guided Scripture)

Legacy Honored

- Madam Hannah Yetunde Ejide Alli-Balogun (1912-1968)

Historical and Family Legacy

- Sheikh Makanjuola Alli-Balogun (Alli-Oloko), Balogun 1 of Lagos (1830-1933)
- Madam Hannah Yetunde Ejide Alli-Balogun, spiritual matriarch (1912-1968)
- Donald Babatunde Coker, brother, mentor, caregiver (1934-2003)
- Anthony Akin Akinbola, brother-in-law, glimpse of paradise (1965-2024)

Churches and Spiritual Communities

- The Apostolic Church Nigeria, 45 Cemetery Street, Lagos
- Household of God Church, Lagos, Nigeria
- Victory Church, Norcross, Atlanta, Georgia
- Citadel Global Community Church (CGCC), Lagos, Nigeria

- Transformation Church, Tulsa, Oklahoma
- Baptist Church, Bradford, England (baptism, 1981)

Songs and Hymns

- "Father, Lead Me Day by Day" (John Hopps)
- "Forth in Thy Name, O Lord I Go" (Charles Wesley)
- "Lead Me Lord" (Gary Valenciano)
- "As the Deer Panteth" (Household of God version)
- "What a God of Mercy He Is" (Household of God Church)
- "Ten Toes" (Rev. Chris Okotie)
- "Faith Talk" (Pastor Michael Todd)
- "Jesus, We Enthrone You" (worship declaration)
- "He'll Send the Word and Make You Whole" (healing anthem)

People and Mentors

- Rev. Chris Okotie, Shepherd Superintendent, Household of God
- Pastor Tunde Bakare, Founding Overseer, CGCC
- Pastor Michael Todd, Transformation Church
- Dr. Fred Tega, encourager
- Sister Teena, Children's Church, Household of God (1987-1999)
- Shola Omojokun, fruit of Children's Church
- Mrs. Mary Coker, counsel, Brighton, England (October 1984)
- Mike Igbokwe SAN, inspirational ministrations
- Jerry Onifade, introduced "Fully Restored" - Pastor Joseph Prince
- Mr. Tayo Ayeni, visits and support
- Ayo Lawson, nourishment and transport, Atlanta
- Bayo Adebowale, emotional support
- Lekan Adebiyi, visits and prayers
- Anne Coker Bremmer, Peju Coker, Biola Balogun, camaraderie & care

Institutions and Milestones

- University of Lagos, monikers (1973-1977)
- University of Bradford, England, Christian Fellowship (1980-1981)
- Porchester Square, London, where Richard met Maureen (1981)
- Holy Cross Cathedral, Lagos, premarital classes and wedding
- Shepherd Center, a catastrophic rehabilitation hospital, Atlanta
- Emory University Hospital Midtown, Spiritual Health Note

Scriptural Anchors

- Ecclesiastes 4:12 (NIV): "A cord of three strands…"
- Job 33:15-16 (KJV): "In a dream… He sealeth their instruction."
- Psalm 145:4-7 (KJV): Generational praise
- Deuteronomy 6:7: Teach them diligently
- Exodus 20:6: Thousand generations
- Psalm 78:6: Children not yet born
- Romans 12:1-2 (KJV): Living sacrifice
- 2 Corinthians 3:2-3 (KJV): Living epistles
- John 6:68 (KJV): Words of eternal life
- Revelation 19:13 (KJV): "His name is called The Word of God."
- Numbers 6:24-26 (KJV): Priestly blessing

www.ingramcontent.com/pod-product-compliance
Lightning Source LLC
LaVergne TN
LVHW041545070426
835507LV00011B/932